The ART and CRAFT of Greeting Cards

Kim K. Stebbins/Maliepaard

The ART and CRAFT of Greeting Cards

A handbook of methods and materials for making and printing greetings, announcements and invitations.

by Susan Evarts

Published by
NORTH LIGHT PUBLISHERS

NORTH LIGHT PUBLISHERS,
an imprint of WRITER'S DIGEST BOOKS,
9933 Alliance Road, Cincinnati, Ohio 45242.

Library of Congress Cataloging in Publication Data

Evarts, Susan.
    The art and craft of greeting cards.

    Bibliography: p.
    1. Greeting cards.   I. Title.
TT872.E93 1975   745.59'4   74-16740
ISBN   0-89134-048-3

Edited by Walt Reed
Designed by Susan Evarts

CHRISTMAS MUMMERS
from Washington Irving's *Old Christmas*, 1878
by Randolph Caldecott

For Allie Owen and the memory of
my Grandmother Barrow and
Grandfather Evarts whose love, wisdom
and wonderful imagination keeps
me faithful to my trade.

Wherever prices of items or services are indicated in the text they represent approximate
prices at the time of writing. Adjustment for
inflation should be considered for accurate
current costs.

ANNUNCIATION TO THE SHEPHERDS
Anonymous woodcut from *Les postilles et
expositions des epistres.* Troyes, 1492

Should this book have any worth, it's due to
the strength and gadfly persistence of my editor
and friend, Walt Reed, who had to make
sense of my phonetic spelling; the exceptional
talents of Looart Studios, George Zariff, and
so many others whose art you'll surely come
to appreciate as much as I do — and of course
to Joe, whose confidence, sensitivity and
domestic assistance made my deadlines possible.
Many Thanks.

CONTENTS

This woodcut, printed in 1450 in the Rhine Valley, Germany, is the earliest known holiday greeting card.

CHAPTER 1
HISTORY

Greetings!

To get off to the right start, I feel we owe our subject some historical attention.

The practice of sending greetings and salutations dates back to the sixth century B.C. when the Egyptians exchanged regards on papyrus scrolls celebrating the advent of the new year. The Chinese and Romans followed suit with messages of felicitation at this season on such materials as scrolls, glazed clay tablets and metal coins or medals.

In medieval Europe, the earliest known holiday card was a crude woodcut printed about 1450 in the Rhine valley of Germany. It was a New Year's card showing the Christ child in the bow of an ancient galley manned by angels, with the Virgin Mary seated by the mast. The inscription states, "Here I come from Alexandria and bring many good years to give generously. I will give them for almost no money and have only God's love for my reward."

But historically it was the Christmas card that really got the tradition started, during the reign of Queen Anne in England (1704-1714). We can attribute part of its origin to the children of this time who wrote "pieces" for their parents and relatives. However, the purpose of these examples was more to show the progress of their penmanship than as intentional salutations. The specimens were written on sheets with engraved borders, some of which had outlined pictures which the children would color in. Another source of the custom stemmed from the adults, who wrote special ornamented Christmas letters to their friends.

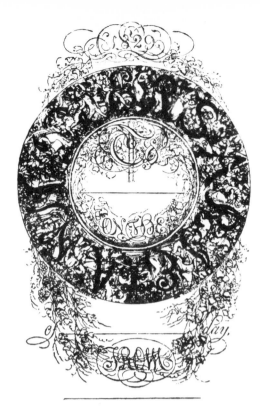

This elaborately engraved anniversary card, dated 1829, could be filled in to serve for Christmas or any other appropriate occasion.

Around 1829, an extremely decorative anniversary card was designed by W. Harvey and engraved by John Thompson. Its message was simply "To   on the Anniversarie of   day from   ." Blank spaces were to be filled in for the appropriate occasion. The first all-purpose card.

The first printed Christmas card, as we know it, must be credited to a very colorful character, Sir Henry Cole, in 1843. Being too busy to write personal greetings to his many friends, he commissioned designer John C. Horsley to create and print a simple black-and-white drawing to convey his best wishes. Incidentally, Sir Cole was a very popular gentleman...about a thousand cards were produced.

In comparison to today's standards, the design was very ornate in style and filled with symbolism. Mr. Horsley created a drawing with a decorative trellis on which is entwined a grapevine forming three panels, two small ones bordering the large central one. The smaller ones show figures representing two acts of charity, "feeding the hungry" and "clothing the naked." In the central picture there is a happy family party, all holding wine glasses filled to the brim. Because of the prudery of the Victorian Era, this particular scene was criticized for encouraging drunkenness and immoral behavior. Fortunately, nothing more serious resulted than some sporadic sputtering.

Running a very close second in time was William Maw Egley, a young engraver's apprentice. In 1848, he designed a very elaborate card depicting his recollection of Happy Christmases gone by. His picture included a family seated around a feast-laden table, a puppet show, a Christmas pantomime and winter skaters. The message, in comparison, was very simple and is still used today:
"A Merry Christmas and a Happy New Year to You".

By 1860, the custom of exchanging cards had become fairly well established throughout the British Empire.

1843 dates the first printed Christmas Card designed by J. C. Horsley at the suggestion and request of his friend Henry Cole.

Even more elaborate in design is Maw Egley's 1848 Christmas Card engraving.

On the home front, Mr. R.H. Pease, a variety storekeeper, should be credited with starting the tradition in Albany, New York, around 1850-52. Rust Craft Publishers apparently has the only known original card. It's interesting to note that Pease was the first to put the Christmas card to a more practical use by combining the holiday greeting with a business advertisement.

However, the man most responsible for the tremendous growth of the American card industry was Louis Prang, historically dubbed "father of the American Christmas card." An exile, following the unsuccessful European revolution of 1848, Prang arrived in New York in 1850 loaded with optimism and determination. He tried a series of short-lived ventures and then set up a small lithographic business in Boston with Julius Mayer. After four years, in 1860, the partnership terminated, leaving the now well-established L. Prang & Co.

Ten persevering years later, he perfected the lithographic process of multicolor printing. The prints were called "chromos." By today's standards, the chromos may be considered poor reproductions of original pictures, but were the best printing possible at that time. We should also credit him with originating the first open competition for Christmas card design in a successful attempt to interest the best contemporary artists. The handsome prizes, ranging from $200 to $1,000, were very motivating.

By the middle 1880's, Prang was printing five million Christmas cards a year. Although he now produced birthday, Easter, New Year's and Valentine cards as well, the Christmas card still accounted for the bulk of his output.

During the 1890's, Prang became discouraged by the competition of a flood of cheap European imports, many simply in post card form, and discontinued that part of his printing business.

Shown above is a typical deluxe creation of Louis Prang. In addition to being fringed and tasseled, these 1880 cards were printed in up to 12 colors.

The woodcut illustration on the right captures the charm of the Victorian Era.

About 1906, an innovation was introduced by Albert Davis of Boston, an importer of German and English cards. Davis' approach to the business created a marked change in both format and contents . . . the sentiment or message was made dominant. Reviewing the form of a hundred years earlier, they were known as Christmas letters. He published his first greeting card using a Dickens verse. It was a very effective format and Davis sold over 500,000 cards the first year he was in business.

Shortly afterwards, Fred and Donald Rust purchased the A.M. Davis Company and continued to build the trade into the still-thriving Rust Craft Company, one of the largest card publishing houses in existence today.

George Gibson arrived in America in the early 1850s. With him, he brought his French-made lithographic press to establish a small family workshop. It wasn't until 1895, however, that Gibson & Co. became the now-famous Gibson Art Co. of Cincinnati. They were first and only distributors of Prang and European cards, but in 1908 they began to produce their own line of Christmas cards.

In 1908, Paul Vollard entered the competition in Chicago. It is believed that his firm was the first to use offset printing for Christmas cards. In 1925, the company was incorporated into the Gerlack-Barklaw Co. in Illinois.

George Buzza's firm produced their first cards (24) in 1909. The designs were simpler, more poster-like, than the previous cards of the time.

Ornate lettering characterizes the Victorian Christmas cards of the 1860's.

Arthur and Jane Norcross, a brother and sister team, started their renowned Norcross Co. in 1914.

Following the Prang tradition, the Hall brothers began their firm in the 1920's. By 1950, the Hallmark Greeting Card Company had become the biggest. Incidentally, the Prang approach was followed not only in style, but also in attracting artists.

Like Prang in the late 1800's, Hallmark staged one of the most successful art contests in France in 1949. Approximately 5,000 artists submitted entries. Ten paintings were selected, and the winners received cash prizes totaling $15,750, plus royalties. A very tidy sum, even by today's standards.

A recent phenomenon has been the "studio" or "contemporary" card, a humorous approach to greetings. This extremely popular form employs the talents of the cartoonist in creating a highly stylized art form. We will get more involved with its history and present effect in a later chapter.

Since Sir Henry Cole's production of 1,000 cards, the growth of the greeting card business has been amazing. In comparison, the present combined annual volume of the 250 card companies in the United States is a staggering 6,000,000,000 . . . half of which are Christmas cards. The postal revenue for such an amount is estimated at over $200,000,000. Retail sale volume is approximately $600,000,000. With figures like these, it seems relatively safe to predict a bright future for anyone engaged in the production or sale of greeting cards . . . so, let's get started.

CHAPTER 2

Ideas

More than half the battle of designing a greeting card is thinking up the idea. Judging from the endless variety of reasons why people send cards, we shouldn't have too much difficulty giving some of our own thoughts visual form. The challenge calls for solid planning, thorough research, a touch of imagination and a lotta' patience.

A good habit to get into is to simply to keep your eyes open and the sketchbook (or large notebook) handy. Learn to jot down everything related to your subject . . . no matter how silly or insignificant it may seem at the time. You would be surprised how some trivia will trigger off a new approach to a well-worn topic.

Take New Year's Eve for example; usually the first thing that pops into one's mind is parties, with confetti, streamers, clocks, horns, drinking, toasting, Father Time, hourglasses, balloons, the New Year's baby, bells, and umpteen others which I'm sure you can add to. The snowballing effect is amazing even after you've settled on a symbol. Let's consider the bell. There are small ones, plain ones, long ones, very decorative ones, loud ones, squat ones, some with handles, others with knobs and still others that swing. Some are gongers, some tinkle, others clang, and so on. This is a good start, but you need not rely entirely on your imagination for the moment. Leave the door open to public and commercial assistance, too.

Museums and libraries are a must. They can be a real source of inspiration. Paintings, sculpture and crafts in museums can be excellent reference. Take advantage of their shops selling postcards, books and pamphlets for additional ideas. The library has books at your disposal covering every subject imaginable. If they have a microfilm file, make use of it. While you're there, browse through the current magazines. Should you find something that sparks an idea, see if your local newsstand still carries it, buy it and clip the reference for your own file.

Most ideas can be quickly visualized with doodles. Here are a few variations of shapes and sizes of bells.

Always make it a point to look in places associated with your subject. Say, for instance, that Father's day is around the corner and you want to surprise him with a personal card. Possibly his favorite hobby is tinkering in the basement and fixing things, so why not look there or at the hardware store for ideas? While rummaging through the nuts and bolts, the old saying "I'm Nuts About You" may pop into mind and there you go. Or you have a friend that's a real bug on sewing. The ideal spot for a bright thought then is the fabric shop, and don't forget to check the notion department for possibilities. The end result may be a card made entirely of material: trim, thread, pins, and so on. Once the idea is there, the rest is all downhill. The important thing to remember is to *look* and keep an *open mind*.

Now's the best time to start making up your own files of research materials. The clippings will consist of most any form of printed media: magazines, newspaper, pamphlets, last year's greeting cards, etc. Pick up about a dozen or so manila folders or envelopes at the stationery

Found materials can suggest ideas too. Here is a unique card made with sandpaper, wire, small nails, nuts and washers, glued to a Bristol board backing.

Cut-out cloth with a strong pattern, thread and heavy knitting yarn, can be combined to make a bright, hand-tailored greeting.

store. Generally categorize your topics to begin with . . . *Animals, Birds, Flowers, Trees and Leaves, Men, Women, Children, Border and Trim, Lettering, Fruits and Vegetables, Holiday Symbols, Costuming, Religious Symbols* . . . these are just a few of the hundreds of possible subjects. You should in some way code each clipping to its folder in case you get involved with two or more subjects. Keep in mind, too, that if you can't find what you want in your own files, large libraries have files on a multitude of topics.

As time goes on, you'll find that collecting, noting, filing and collating ideas is not only an interesting, but a rewarding process. It helps to stimulate your imagination and increase your thinking capacity.

Don't panic if your mind draws a blank or has a dry spell. It happens to everybody, more often than you think. The best thing then is to drop the whole procedure. Let it be! Do something else! Much to your surprise, the idea will come to you when you least expect it.

Let the event spark the idea. What could be more appropriate than to use cards from a discarded deck to make personalized invitations for bridge?

4 IN 1 PARTY:
BRIDGE
SNACKS
DRINKS
& FUN

SUN. 14TH 1:00

HOPE YOU
MAKE IT

A few final suggestions. Give yourself time to think up ideas. Go for a long walk (weather permitting), curl up in a quiet corner or, as I do, haunt the areas correlated with your subject.

When a thought comes to mind, make a quick sketch of it. Thinking in *visual* terms may seem awkward to begin with, but it's the best way to organize your ideas.

Never be satisfied with the first idea that occurs to you. Do several. This is based on the same principle as jotting down ideas. The greater the variety of sketches you have, the better the chance of coming up with a terrific new idea.

And finally, make it a point to keep up with new trends, new materials, new printing processes, etc. They can certainly add to your sources of ideas and techniques.

A single idea can be interpreted in endless ways. Here the theme of rebirth is charmingly expressed in two variations.

Below. Here is just a sampling of some thirty different Santas made as a Christmas greeting for Publishers Graphic's Studios by their artist members. Try your own version!

"THERE IS NOTHING I CAN GIVE YOU
WHICH YOU HAVE NOT,
BUT THERE IS MUCH, VERY MUCH,
THAT WHILE I CANNOT GIVE IT,
YOU CAN TAKE..."

Courtesy, Publishers Graphics

An example of a hinged pop-up card as described on page 24.

20

CHAPTER 3
PAPERS

Paper is definitely one of the most important materials used in greeting card designing. Grain, weight, surface texture, color, and finish will each be a contributing factor to the effectiveness of your card. Even standard paper sizes and cutting information should become a consideration for economy purposes. Listed below are some of the most commonly used paper stocks for printing:

CONSTRUCTION — Soft fibrous, rough finish paper; available in a variety of colors.

CHARCOAL — Rather coarse surface paper: also in many colors.

VELLUM — Semi-smooth paper with an excellent surface for drawing or wash.

RICE PAPER — This term covers a variety of Japanese handmade papers; color is generally from white to buff.

PARCHMENT — A high grade paper made to simulate a genuine parchment or thin, translucent animal skin.

COATED — This term covers a wide range of papers, both in weight and color. They have been coated with a solution to produce a very smooth surface.

BRISTOLS — These are papers of post card weight or more. Made to take ink and erasing well. Various finishes available.

Of these, I suggest the construction paper to get you started. It's cheap and takes well to most forms of printing. In the long run though, I especially recommend the *Bristols*. My preference is Strathmore Beau Brilliant, Strathmore Text, Grandee and Fiesta, in that order. For a quiet, subtle color range, consider Strathmore's Pastelle or Chroma. Samples may be found at your local stationery or art supply stores.

For that very special touch, you might also look into their reversible stock, one side being colored or tinted while the other remains white or is still another color.

In addition to these stand-bys, there are other papers that have distinct characteristics all their own. Foil or metallic paper, for instance, has a bright laminated surface, available in numerous weights. Very similar is fluorescent paper, coated with highly luminous color. In contrast consider a velour paper stock, with its soft fur-like texture made with either cotton or rayon fibers or the smooth satiny coated Color-Aid paper in a huge selection of hues and tones.

Even wrapping paper, wallpaper, and contact paper offer possibilities worth investigating. However, hold off on these novelties until you become more familiar with the idiosyncrasies of printing. Stick to those recommended for now. Also consider light pastel colors . . . yellows, pinks, pale blues and greens, violets, tans, etc., since it's easier to print a dark ink or paint on a light surface than vice-versa.

A characteristic you should always be aware of in all machine-made paper is the grain or direction of the paper fibers. These make tearing and folding in one direction easier than in the other. Plan the fold of your card to run in its favor. A simple method of checking the grain is the fold test. Paper that is folded with the grain gives a more uniformly smooth crease. In going against the grain, the fold is rough and tends to crack or break down the fibers.

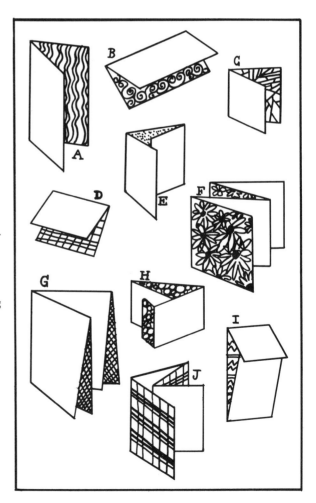

FOLDS

A number of popular folds are illustrated on this chart. Fig. A—4-page, 1 fold, upright, narrow or slim card. Fig. B—4-page, 1 fold, upright to be used lengthwise. Fig C—4-page, 1 fold, upright, wide card. Fig. D— 4-page, 1 fold, upright to be used lengthwise. Fig. E— 6-page, 2 parallel folds. Fig. F—8-page, 3 accordion folds. Fig. G— 8-page 2 fold, called French fold when printing is on one side of the paper. Fig. H—6-page with flap, 3 parallel folds. Fig. I—4-page with flap, 2 parallel folds, oblong. Fig. J—8-page, 2 parallel folds.

There are, of course, many other folds and you will enjoy originating your own. Always remember to fold in the same direction as the grain on cards with one fold.

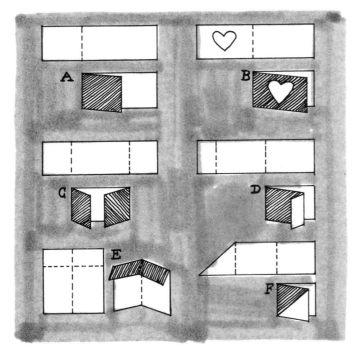

A. The simplest and most obvious reversible paper fold is an off-center crease. When folded, the bottom fold extends beyond the top fold.

B. The reversible paper has been folded in the middle. A design has been cut out of the top fold thus allowing the bottom fold color to show through.

C. The same principle used in Fig. A is used for this card, with the exception that two folds are made rather than one. The center opening then exposes the second color.

D. This fold employs the modified French fold, the exterior side being deeper than the interior side so that both colors are exposed on the interior of the card.

E. This card is folded so that the two right-hand portions of the card are equal. The remaining short section of the inside color is then folded back across a portion of the cover.

F. This card is folded into three equal parts, with a diagonal cut made on the extreme left portion. When folded, the card will appear as shown.

There are, of course, many interesting and original folds that can be created with the reversible paper, and it would be well worth your time to experiment in making original folds of your own.

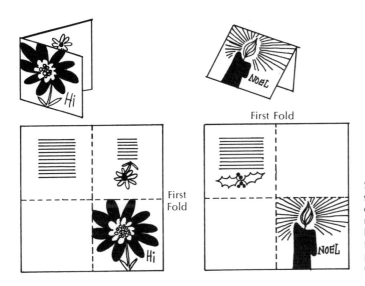

First Fold

First Fold

Shown at left are two cards of the French fold type. The sketches are self-explanatory and indicate placement of art work and message in relation to the two folds necessary to make this card. Variations can, of course, be made on the inside pages. The back page of the folded card, however, should be left blank. The paper stock should not be too heavy, otherwise the card will be too bulky.

When buying pre-folded cards, there is no grain problem as it has already been determined. However, if ordering large quantities of greeting card stock, your best bet is to put the order through a printer and let him know how you plan to cut and fold it, so you can be reasonably sure that he'll order the right size and grain to fit the job.

Now that we're aware of the grain, let's give some thought to the various kinds of folds you can make. Here again you should take some time to observe the market. Notice how some folds will enhance the character of your sentiment.

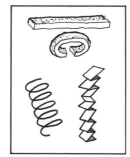

Spring devices used for pop-up and jump cards.

Hinged Pop-Up

A. Fold card in half. Fold tab at bottom and twice at top as shown. Be sure lengths between top two folds and bottom fold are the same.

B. Cement bottom fold to lower part of card. Bring top part of card to vertical position and glue to upper fold of tab.

C. Secure separate motif to remaining long portion of tab.

Center Fold Pop-Up

A. Using lightweight card stock, fold card in half. Lightly draw two lines approximately one inch from center fold and equally spaced. Gently score lines and fold inward.

B. Cement motif to center fold as shown.

Platform Pop-Up

A. Make the platform tab of stiff bristol board. With a pencil, mark the center to line up with the center fold of the card and then indicate the two end folds one half and one inch accordingly. Fold and cement the very end folds to card as demonstrated. B. Be sure platform is cemented exactly over the center of the card. This also applies when attaching the motif to the card, otherwise it will not fold properly.

Something as corny as "Only you deserve a real DOG of a card" could be accompanied by an elongated decorative dachshund-type dog on an accordian fold. Shown before are a number of other popular folds to experiment with, the most familiar being the French fold. This double fold gives a more sumptuous appearance and it suggests to the recipient an added expense. In fact it is less expensive, since it allows all of the printing to be done on one side of the sheet. In addition, this means that a lighter (and cheaper) paper stock can be used since the two folds gave the necessary sturdiness. The normal single fold stock would be too bulky.

A little more complicated in construction are the pop-up and jump cards. They usually require hinges, platforms, easel-type supports and various spring devices. With just a bit more effort, you can really let the recipient in for a snazzy unusual surprise. The obvious extra time also reflects your feelings for him or her . . . that special touch. Three simple pop-up methods you might try are the center fold pop-up, platform pop-up, and the hinged pop-up. Rely on a hefty stock for the pop-up shapes, platforms and hinges. The actual card stock, however, may vary in weight depending on the complexity of the construction.

The "jump-up" term is really self explanatory. Small pictorial shapes are cemented to a spring or similar device which allows them to pop out when the card is opened. One such device is a thin strip of foam rubber, approximately 2" x ½" x ⅛" simply coiled and cemented to the inside flap of the card. The graphic shape is then pasted on the foam rubber. Coiling a lightweight wire for the spring jump-up isn't that difficult. I recommend a sturdy household glue, either Duco or Elmer's to guarantee adhesion. The final mechanism is an accordian jump-up. You recall the

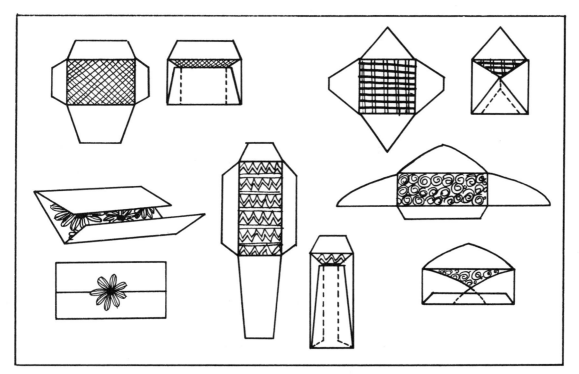

Here are some basic envelope shapes and folds. Select one that suits the size of your card and make a cardboard pattern of the open shape for easier transfer and cutting. Fold envelopes over a piece of cardboard cut at least ⅛" larger than your card, then cement the edges with rubber cement.

accordian fold illustrated on page 23 . . . same principle.
All you require is a 4-5" x ½" stiff piece of paper, fold
in accordion fashion, glue to card and object, and . . . voila! These are the basics, but don't let them stop you from devising your own 3-D prop. There are a multitude of possibilities.

ENVELOPES

It's important that you plan the size and shape of your card thoughtfully, as it will have to be determined by the dimensions of the envelope. Becoming familiar with the standard stationery sizes will have an influence on the proportions you make your card. Your card should be ¼" narrower than the envelope width, and ⅛" shorter than the depth. The general envelope sizes you'll discover, are 4 ⅜" x 5 ⅜", 5 ¼" x 7", 4 ¾" x 6 ½", on up. The long narrow envelopes are about 3 ¾" x 8 ⅛". For larger sizes, it would be wise to insert one or two firm pieces of cardboard to avoid damage during delivery. Most of these standards are available in a variety of colors and textures at the art supply or stationery stores.
If you are not satisfied with color alone, why not add a nice individual touch by printing a simple pattern . . . possibly a border or corner motif?

When producing large quantities of cards, I'd suggest sticking to the commercial sizes for economic and expedient purposes. But for those special occasions, consider making your own envelopes. It's not difficult and the wide assortment of colored papers, patterns and printing techniques you can combine, make for endless possibilities. The inside of the card or liner, for instance, could be a mad flower motif while the outside could be a contrasting stripe or polka-dot pattern. Take advantage of the previously mentioned paper stocks. Better yet, let your imagination run the gamut . . . select your own combination.

An eraser stamp helps to add a novel touch to your envelopes. Also gives the recipient a hint of what's inside.

An easy central slit made at opposite sides of the cake panels produced the dimensional card that went with the envelope.

The construction procedure can be done in one of two ways. First you can use a standard envelope as a guide. Carefully pull the flaps apart, lay it flat on your envelope paper, trace the shape, cut, fold and glue. Or you may try one of the examples shown for starters. When measuring the card for envelope proportions, be sure to allow at least an ⅛" margin so that it will slip in easily. Once measured and the dimensions lightly drawn, cut the shape with scissors. To ensure a neat straight crease, score the fold lines with a blunt knife, an envelope opener, or a metal ruler. Now simply fold and glue the edges with rubber cement. Since the postal service takes a grim view of triangular or other odd-shaped envelopes, it would be wise to restrict yourself to square or rectangular shapes.

As a change of pace, you can depart from the envelope altogether by considering mailing tubes. These are perfect for large poster sized cards. The recipient is not only pleased with the unique mailing package, but the creaseless card besides . . . very impressive presentation. Check the telephone yellow pages for size and buying details.

Finally, don't forget the self-mailers, the card simply folded up, sealed and addressed. As a break or a real quickie, you can eliminate the card shape completely by putting your graphics and message on the inside of the envelope. Top it off with an attractive seal sold at the art or stationery store or make your own in simple shape that will reflect the receiver's personality or the event.

The accordian fold is not only simple to make, but versatile. One approach is to print or illustrate your design on the outside of the card, put the message on the inside. Carefully fold inward allowing the flaps to overlap, then glue a pretty tag motif to seal an unusual self mailer.

Remember those simple snowflake designs you used to make way back when by cutting through a many folded piece of construction paper? The same technique was used for this card. The cut out paper was then mounted on a bright contrasting foil wrapping paper.

TEXTURES

There is such a wide variety of paper stocks on the market with distinctive enough surface textures and patterns that you shouldn't have too much difficulty in finding what you want to work with.

Going a step further, should you want a paper pattern or texture other then what is commercially made, once again you can devise your own. A word of caution, however. Although it occupies a secondary role, background pattern can give life and vitality to your design . . . as well as ruin it if not chosen and executed wisely. Always remember that it's the motif and greeting that is the purpose of your card. The background texture should enhance . . . complement these elements . . . never conflict with them.

The techniques described and illustrated on these pages can be easily mastered, and used individually or in combinations. Their effects and variations are limitless, and I'm sure it won't be long before you're adding many more to the ones suggested here.

Now, let's experiment with making your own colored paste papers. One easy and inexpensive texture is achieved by combining white library paste with watercolor. The paste must be quite free from lumps (strained if necessary) and of medium consistency.

If it is too thick there will be danger of it flaking off the paper when it dries. Mix with the paste about a third to half as much watercolor, poster color, or dye. Brush the mixture over the paper and, while still wet, you will be able to make a variety of imprints. . .using jar lids, wide-tooth combs, fingers, sides and ends of pencils, just to name a few possible tools.

Making imitation parchment paper is just as easy . . . on you and on the pocketbook. Next time you happen to be in the stationery store, pick up some 16 pound typewriter paper of good quality. Pour a small amount of cooking or salad oil in a saucer, then lightly dab both sides of the paper with a soft clean cloth. Junior's old diapers can really come in handy now. Allow the paper to dry for several days. That's all there is to it.

Toothbrush

Sponge

Stamp

Spatter

Inkblot

Cap Stamps

Kleenex

29

DECKLE EDGE

Some stocks come with a decorative trim called a deckle edge. This is the soft feathery end of a machine- made paper stock usually clipped off in the final production process. However, many bristols will retain the edge for a more elegant expensive touch.

Handmade paper comes with a feathery deckle edge on all four sides, unless trimmed. Machine-made paper has a deckle edge on two opposite sides until trimmed. The deckling runs with the grain on machine-made paper and occurs when the paper fibers at the edge of the web try to flow under the rubber dam or deckle that determines the width of the paper.

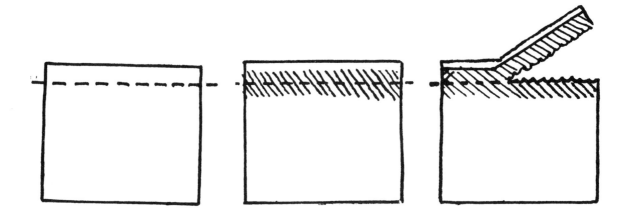

MAKING YOUR OWN DECKLE EDGE

To save a few pennies, you might consider making your own deckle edge. It's simpler than you think. I suggest a fairly soft but hefty paper . . . Rice and construction papers make terrific deckle edges. On a sheet of paper, before cutting it, draw a faint line with a ruler to mark the edge that is to be deckled. Take a paint brush and saturate with water a strip about one quarter inch wide on either side of the line. Turn the paper and repeat the process. Once completely saturated, put a ruler on the pencil line and tear upward. Remove the ruler and smooth out the edges with your fingers. You have a deckled edge! Allow the paper to dry before using, however.

One of the most available tools for creating an unusual background pattern is your own hand. Dip your forefinger and/or thumb in ink or tempera, and then press on a hard, smooth-surfaced paper. This will surely produce a pattern to impress any police department. Vary the degree of over-printing for a wider value range.

Toothpicks and paper clips can produce a nice contrast of thick and thin lines. Dipping some in thick paint and others in a much thinner paint can also add variation.

The kitchen holds an amazing assortment of neat texture-making tools. This one was done with an inexpensive bamboo trivet and tempera. But don't overlook forks, jar caps, doilies, the broom or even the scrub brush. One of my favorite texture makers is an old-fashioned potato masher.

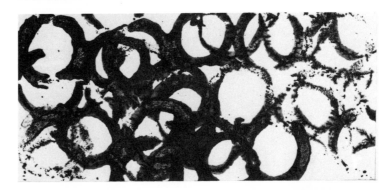

For a soft, blended background, try a wet-in-wet technique with tempera, ink, or watercolor. Dampen the paper surface, then add your paint. Experiment by varying light and dark colors. While the paint is still slightly damp, you can take the side or point of a razor blade and scrape into the surface for still more variation.

Crayon on a rough, nubbly paper surface is great for just that kind of texture—rough and nubbly. The amount of pressure placed on the crayon will determine the degree of texture and value.

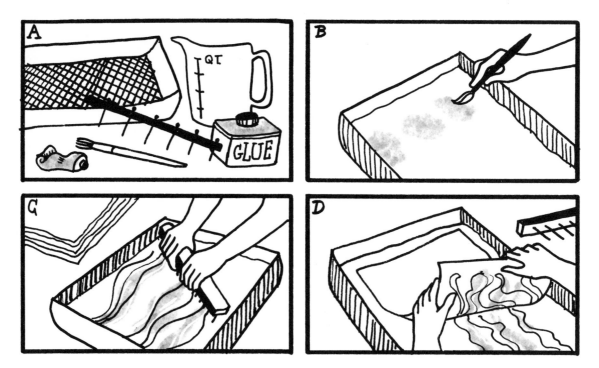

A) The assembled materials for method No. 2, should also include a wood stick or thick cardboard strip punctured with small finishing nails at approximately 1-inch intervals to form a comb.

B) Spots of color are dropped on surface of the glue-size solution in tray.

C) Using nail stick comb or sharp end of brush, draw it through the color spots to create marbled patterns.

D) Lay paper on surface, lift off, and hang to dry.

MARBLING

Method No. 1

Into a tray of boiling hot water drop razor thin slices of different colored crayons. Let them melt. Stir the water a little, but not enough to mix the colors completely. Then put a sheet of paper on top of the water, or roll it across if it is too large, and remove it at once. Put the paper on a wooden table or a block of wood and fasten the corners with thumbtacks while it dries. This will keep the paper from curling.

Method No. 2

Marbling with oil colors - you will need oil colors, brushes, and a waterproof tray, bowl or pan large enough to hold the paper to be marbled.

Any paper with a fairly porous surface may be used.

Into the tray pour warm water (or better, weak solution of size, 1 teaspoonful of powder glue to each quart of water) to a depth of about one inch. Allow to stand until it is at room temperature. Cut several pieces of stout paper 2 or 3 inches wide and the length of the tray.

Mix colors to a thin dropping consistency with turpentine in separate containers and have a brush for each color.

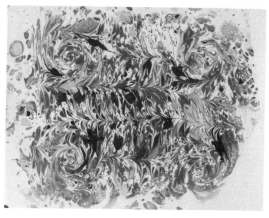

One of the most exciting aspects of marbling is that no two patterns are alike. Once started, you'll be surprised how much paper you'll go through just to see what the next pattern will be like.

When the size or water is quite still, drop spots of color onto the surface in regular positions over the tray. The spots should each spread to a width of 3 or 4 inches. If they do not spread sufficiently more turps should be added to the color. If the spots spread very rapidly and too much, add more color to the mixture. If the color sinks to the bottom of the tray, the size is too thick and more water must be added.

Draw the colors slowly and carefully into patterns with the stick or end of a brush. Take care not to disturb the water too much or all control of the patterns will be lost.

When the water is again still, take the piece of paper in both hands and lower it gradually onto the surface of the water, putting it down first at one end of the tray and gradually lowering it to the other end. This is to prevent air being trapped between paper and water, resulting in a blank space in the pattern. When the paper floats on the surface of the water lift it slowly from one end to drain off the water and hang to dry. When dry it may be varnished or polished with a warm iron.

Take a strip of paper and skim the surface of the water to remove any specks of color before repeating the process.

In addition to these, you can create many unusual background patterns simply by applying paint with ordinary objects to be found around the home: pipe cleaners, old toothbrushes, sponges, crumpled paper tissues or paper towelling, string, corks, broom straws, etc. The effects to be achieved in using these articles are somewhat unpredictable, but in testing each one you will get a fair idea of the pattern that will result. Work with a minimum number of colors to begin with and be sure to allow each color to dry before superimposing another on top of it. As for media, I suggest experimenting with tempera colors, transparent watercolors, colored inks, block print inks, etc. Also experiment with a wide range of papers to see how much the textural appearance of each technique will vary.

Before starting, you should protect your working table with a layer of old newspapers, then place a smooth sheet of cardboard on top to serve as a work surface. Arrange all printing materials, media, tools, small bowl for water, paper, etc., conveniently around your working surface.

CHAPTER 4
LETTERING AND VERSE

LETTERING

Many artists consider this phase of card designing to be the most tedious, uncreative part. Not so! It all depends on how you tackle it. I have friends who relish the meticulous mechanics of spacing and proportions. If you happen to be one of these people, you're in an enviable position. However, if you are like me and lack the necessary patience, good eye and steady hand, don't despair. There are several ways out. You may solve the entire lettering problem by designing a card without any lettered greeting on the front. Simply write a personal message on the back of a single card or on the inside of a folded card.

However, with just a little tenacity and mechanical help, you may be surprised at how proficient at lettering you really can be. One suggestion to get you started is to select a commercially printed card (or any printed material) with a style of lettering that appeals to you. Pick several. Trace the letters till you learn the shapes of them. Try recombining them to get a feel for the spacing. Make it a habit to clip and file all kinds of lettering; you never know when you may have a use for it.

Now that you've gained enough confidence, try a few of your own variations. Just remember that readability is essential. No matter how much you distort the character of the letter form ALWAYS retain the features that make it legible. Try to select a style of lettering that will reflect the nature of your subject. Should the greeting or invitation be a very formal one, consider a simple script style of lettering, possibly in italic. If the occasion be in a lighter vein, you may want to use a heftier, more irregular fun-type style. Sometimes you can create lettering that will visually describe the event. Say, for example, you're in the mood to renovate . . . why not have a small group of friends over for a paint party, free beer and snacks, etc. Paint the letters as you would the wall. Use a half inch flat brush, leave the edges rough and streaky for that painty look.

This was a fast, fun way to paint
an invitation and gets the event off
on the right foot.

Letters cut out of little circular-
shaped pieces of styrofoam,
then stamped with acrylics, created this simple ornament-
tree version. Irregular placement
of the letters appears more
spontaneous and festive.

Or if you can in some way combine the letter forms with your pictorial shape,
better yet. This approach not only makes your design unique, but helps it to work
more visually as a whole. You saw an example of this in the
previous chapter . . . the stencil cut greeting "Happy New Year"
had been carefully shaped to create a bell. The main thing to keep in mind with
this procedure is to KEEP IT SIMPLE. Avoid complicated symbols.
Otherwise, the lettering could easily become unreadable.

At this point I feel it's only fair to mention the lettering guide sets and other
mechanical devices. These require a nominal amount of skill or experience.
In all honesty, I must admit that I find them very stiff, limited and
unimaginative, especially the commercial stencil set. Very personal and
decorative lettering can be created by cutting your own stencils, as we'll discuss
in a later chapter. Wrico, Doric, Leroy and other similar lettering sets are a
little more complex. They consist of templates on which the
selected letters or symbols are incised. Included is a pen and scriber which trace
the letters from the template. The styles available are simple sans serif letters
which can be fairly rapidly formed once you get the hang of it.

A better answer may be found in transfer lettering, under such trade
names as "Letraset," "Formatt," "Zip-a-tone," "Artype" and "Prestype." This is
a more recent process which makes possible the transferring of
letters or complete words directly on your card. Such traditionals as Merry
Christmas, Happy New Year, Greetings of the Season, etc.,
are printed on transparent plastic sheets.When rubbed gently, the words are
neatly transferred to the card. If you feel more adventuresome, there are
also whole alphabets available in a variety of styles and colors. You

Commercial diecut stencil guides provide one fast, useful method of lettering.

These individual stencil letters on metal plates can be taken apart and reassembled as needed.

Wrico lettering guides require no more skill or experience than the other stencil guides. The Wrico pen is moved in contact with the sides of the guide to form letters and numerals.

just have to be a little more careful lining up and spacing the letters since you're making the word yourself. Besides the instant lettering, there are transfer borders, textures, patterns, tones, and symbols to cover most any general subject. Prices range from $1.00 - $4.00, depending on the size and complexity of the transfer. Most relatively large art stores will at least carry a catalog if not a moderate supply of transfer products. A word of caution, however. Once transferred the letterforms may crack or chip off if the card is roughly handled. A light coating of spray fixative would help reinforce it.

The ultimate in lettering convenience, however, is to use preprinted cards. You simply take a packet of blank cards (next chapter) to the local printer or typesetter with a sketch of what you have in mind. When returned, complete your paste-up or free hand drawing above or below the printed greeting. My objection to this procedure is that it's a bit expensive, takes part of the fun out of creating the whole card, and it minimizes that personal touch.

Finally, should you really want to get into the mechanics of good lettering, by all means do so. You can't help but benefit from the experience. Once again, take advantage of the library for some good "how-to" books.

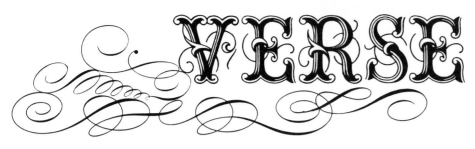

VERSE

I'm sure you've discovered at one time or another that knowing what you want to say and saying it simply and personally are two different things. If you happen to be poetically inclined . . . more power to you. However, if you're more artistic than literary, more perseverance and a little outside help is needed. Such reference material as John Bartlett's *Familiar Quotations* or *5,000 Quotations for All Occasions* could really come in handy. Should you have something definite in mind, there are quotation books on the Bible, Shakespeare, love, humor, wisdom etc. Most of these can be found in the library. Also check out Clement Wood's *The Complete Rhyming Dictionary.* The introduction will give you all you need to know on the basics of versification. In fact, browse through it when not actually using it. It may produce an inspiration for a verse. For reference on structure, be it meter or free verse, consider the following publications:

> *Writing Light Verse* by Richard Armour,
>   Publisher, The Writer, Inc., Boston

> *Writing and Selling of Greeting Card Verse* by June Barr
>   Publisher, The Writer, Inc., Boston

> *Greeting Card Magazine,* New York, N.Y.

I especially recommend Carl Goeller's *Selling Poetry, Verse, and Prose* Doubleday & Co., the author being a former editor-in-chief of Rust Craft Greeting Cards.

A word regarding the technical side of versification . . . Keep it simple and distinct. Nothing takes the place of good grammar. Try to avoid overused words, a trite verse will make a trite card. However, be generous with the pronoun "you", it has that magic personal touch. Should the occasion call for a Victorian vernacular such as "thee" or "thou", spice with some contemporary language . . . maybe something like "My Ticker Doth Palpitate". Develop a conversational tone . . . be expressive, personal and to the point. Don't be sidetracked by 2 or 3 different ideas . . . a single thought for one verse. Work to keep it short and meaningful. In order for your phrase to be effective it should touch the person who receives it . . . make him feel happy or tender, sentimental or surprised, loved or appreciated or something. Believe me, a cold piece of copy has no appeal. Sometimes it's helpful to conjure a mental image of the "special" person or an equivalent while developing your message. It makes it easier to establish that personal feeling.

Finally, learn to develop the same research and filing habits for verse as you have for your artwork. Those 3" x 5" or 4" x 6" file cards are great for jotting down thoughts and phrases. Along with your sketchpad, why not carry a small note book . . . you never know when a literary gem may be triggered off by some incident or routine event.

Lettering is an integral part of a design. Its styles or character should reflect the purpose of the card.

Dry transfer sheets of lettering in various sizes and styles, as well as decorative designs and symbols are available in most local art supply stores. With them you can easily transfer the lettering to almost any surface, and a spacing guide printed beneath the letters permits accurate spacing and lineup.

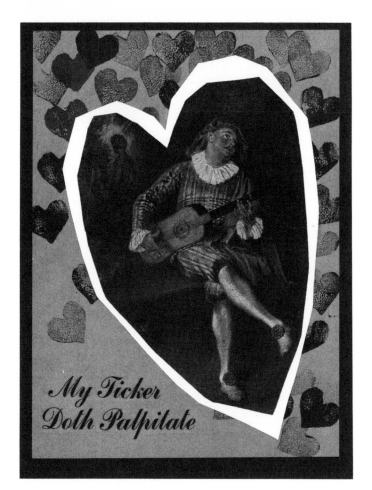

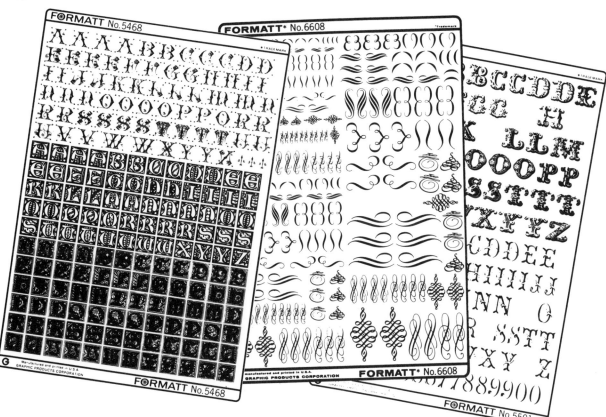

CHAPTER 5

Now that your head is swarming with a terrific variety of ideas and materials, I think it's time we started applying them. Let's begin in low gear with a "monoprint." This process is simply what the name implies — one print. Each print is different from the previous one, making it an original. To the recipient of your card, this is a very special thing. Yet, the printing procedure is very simple and calls for a minimum of skill and equipment. I recommend printing ink or oil paints for their longer drying time rather than water-based paints such as acrylics, poster paints, or watercolor. You'll want plenty of time to paint in your shapes and print, especially if you're covering a relatively large area.

The first step is to sketch out your idea on tracing paper. It should be made the same size as your intended print. Go easy on detail; shapes ought to be kept as simple and well defined as possible. This is most important as you will be printing your design directly on the plate. Keep in mind that it will be a little difficult to confine the shapes exactly to your sketch while printing. As a result, the final print will be a looser, more spontaneous version of the original drawing. You'll see what I mean when we get going. Right now let's concentrate on those simple shapes: a shamrock, perhaps, for St. Patrick's Day or a firecracker to announce your Fourth of July picnic or make use of candles, fir trees and stars to convey the Christmas spirit, and so on. On your sketch, be sure to fill in the areas that will be printed. This way you have a better idea of how the print will appear.

The printing procedure can be done in one of two ways, either with acetate film or glass, depending on which is the handiest. For the first, and my preference, you'll need a piece of medium to heavy weight acetate, about 5 to 6 inches larger than the area you're going to print, oil paints or printing ink (keep the number of colors to a minimum to start with, about two or three), a small to medium-sized watercolor brush, a few sheets of relatively absorbent paper such as construction or Bristol, turpentine, clean rags, masking tape, and a large table or floor area to work on.

If you are using the printing ink, a light dusting of talcum powder on the acetate will give the surface a slight tooth, helping the ink to adhere better. It is also possible, but not necessary, to purchase "prepared" acetate which is specially coated on both sides to take any medium without beading or crawling. A single 14" x 17" sheet runs about 65¢, a pad of twelve sheets is about $8.00. Besides these tools, you'll naturally need sketch and tracing pads, pencils, erasers, etc. Also, be sure your card paper is cut to size. Now that we've got everything, let's go.

Once the sketch is completed, turn it over and trace it on the back so you can make your printing plate a reverse image. (Then when you print from the acetate onto your paper, it will come out with the correct picture, reading the right way.) Place the acetate sheet on top and paint in your shapes using the sketch underneath as a guide. While it is still wet, lift the acetate, turn it over, and place gently on your paper stock. Apply hand

1) Make sketch on tracing paper
2) Reverse, trace on back, tack down with tape, place and secure acetate on top.
3) Paint image on acetate.
4) Lift, place acetate upside down on printing paper. Secure and rub image carefully. Remove and let dry.
5) And . . . *Voila!*

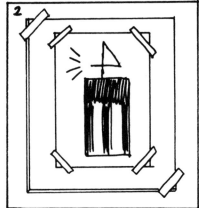

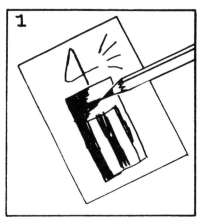

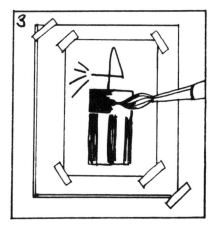

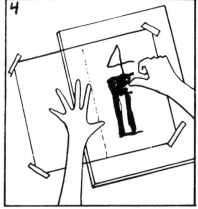

pressure gingerly so as not to force the paint to spread out beyond the original shapes too much. Just before removing the acetate plate, you may want to create a scratch-like texture with your fingernail, comb, fork, or other pointed object. If your design includes leaves, for example, it's a great way to create a veined pattern, or to make a checkerboard treatment for a dress fabric, or possibly a radiating linear pattern to emphasize sun or candlelight. I'm sure you'll come up with many others. Now carefully lift the acetate from the card, wipe or rinse clean and begin the process all over again.

The second procedure is very similar to the previous one. We simply substitute a piece of window glass or clear plastic of the same weight for the acetate and reverse the last part of the printing operation. Follow the same step-by-step procedure, but instead of putting the plate on the card, do the opposite.

Place the paper on the glass or plastic. Secure the paper at one end with masking tape so it won't shift, rub gently, score a texture with your fingernail or other pointed object if you wish, then carefully remove. Wipe the glass or plastic clean as you did with the acetate and start anew.

There is still one other monoprint method that eliminates the printing plate altogether. I'm sure you remember those ink blot designs used for the analysis of personality, more commonly known as the Rorschach test. Blobs of ink are placed on one side of a folded piece of paper, which is pressed together and opened again to create a duplicate pattern on the other side. Same principle. But instead of making the print a one-time thing you can do it in stages.

All you have to do is lightly pencil a design on one side of the card. Once again, keep the shapes simple. Now simply color one shape, close, carefully press with fingers to make the duplicate image, open, paint the next shape, close and so on. Since this is a shape-by-shape procedure, water-based paints can be used. When you've finished the duplication, allow the print to dry, then reverse the fold. The pattern should then appear on the front and back of the card. This process is particularly useful for designs that call for repetition, such as a sexagenarian birthday card or a "two heads are better than one" sort of thing. It's a fast and easy printing method to keep in mind when there's no time to lose.

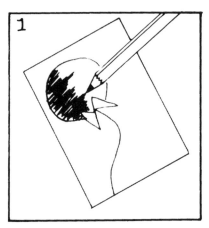

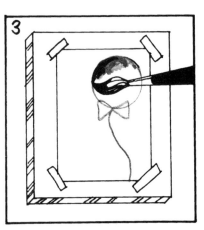

1) Make sketch on tracing paper.

2) Reverse, trace on back, tack down with tape, and place glass on top.

3) Paint image on glass.

4) Now, carefully place card paper on top of glass and rub gingerly. Remove and let dry.

5) If desired, paint in message and additional detail.

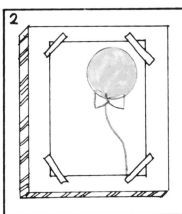

One final word of encouragement. Don't give up the ship if the first few prints don't come off. You should make a batch of trial prints to be sure the consistency of your paint and the hand pressure applied is just right. Also try to avoid piling your paint on too thickly. Otherwise it will spread too much during the printing process, making your shapes unrecognizable.

Once you get the hang of it, you should experiment with many different paints, inks, and paper stocks. You might even want to make a background texture before printing, possibly with a sponge or stamp. Or consider overprinting with still another print. The acetate plate has a unique texture all its own after printing and would certainly make for a handsome, individual card. Or, why not mount and frame it for yourself?

After a few more chapters, it won't be long before you're combining this printing method with others — like stamps, for a starter.

Flowers provide a fun subject for Rorschach-monoprinting. Be sure to put enough paint on the first image so that the printed image will be as distinct.

Shown on the preceding page are just a few of the limitless varieties of found objects that can be used in stamp printing. The challenge is in finding them.

The most convenient place to start looking is right around the house — sewing spools and buttons, sponges, bottle tops and jar lids, combs, doilies, clothes pins, cooking utensils and so on. The local hardware and variety stores will contribute such inexpensive possibilities as screening, scrub and paint brushes, those precut uniform patterns for wood and metal make-it-yourself dividers (ask for the odd size remnants, they're cheaper), decorative molding, string and rope, cosmetic and costume sundries, giftware and novelty goods, etc.

Nature, too, provides a good assortment. A block of very grainy wood will create a nice spontaneous linear pattern and leaves come in all shapes and sizes (try to select those with strong protruding veins for a more distinct print). And don't overlook the pantry and supermarket. The spiral grooves on the plastic backing for supermarket meat create a terrific radiating effect — useful for suns, stars, candlelight and halos. A halved onion can produce a very delicate lacy flower print (allowing it to dry out a day will create a more textural print and be less malodorous). Cabbage and tomatoes should also be considered. And if you can afford it, half a head of fresh broccoli makes a very neat tree shape, as in "Happy Arbor Day."

A. Squeeze paint onto glass, enamel or plastic slab. Roll brayer or roller to coat.

B. Apply to found object stamp.

C. Or, use a more direct approach and apply paint directly from the tube or jar with a brush.

D. Now stamp away.

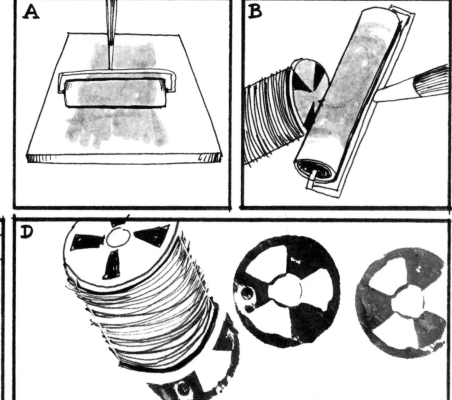

When you have assembled the ready-made objects you are going to use, carefully plan what kind of pattern you want to make. It's not a bad idea to roughly sketch out the placement of your prints on another sheet of paper to give yourself an indication of how it will look. I would suggest a fairly absorbent paper for printing to minimize blotches and paint build-up around the tool. Construction paper or an inexpensive Bristol will suffice to begin with.

Poster, tempera, acrylic and oil paints, colored inks and stamp pads are generally used as coloring materials. Media can be applied two ways:

1) Paint or ink is first applied on an enamel tray, a glass or a plastic slab, then rolled on to printing tool; or,
2) Apply paint directly to the object with a wide (½'' at least) nylon brush. They're cheap and quite durable.

Try to keep the consistency of your paint or ink like medium cream. You risk an incomplete, blotchy print if the mixture is too thick. If it is too thin, the print will appear blurred. Keeping a test sheet on the side is a good way to check the results.

The side of a head of broccoli, dipped in paint, created a replica of a miniature tree when printed on paper. The shape of the bag and the lettering were added for the base. The design is reproduced in color on page 127.

Now that we've explored found objects as printing tools, let's consider some homemade relief prints. One of the easiest to cut and most accessible is the potato. Very simple shapes and patterns would be best. Needless to say, because it is perishable, it should be used immediately; life expectancy is about two days, on the outside.

The printing procedure is very simple. First select a firm potato of medium size. Wash and dry it before cutting in half. Then with a small brush and ink or magic marker, carefully outline your design. If lettering, remember to make the characters backwards since the finished print will appear in reverse. Now, with a sharp paring or jack-knife, cut away the undesired area, leaving the raised portion for printing about ¼" high. The cuts of the design should be slanted slightly *outward* to give it a solid base. The paint can be applied as demonstrated for the found-object tools. The final step is to simply press the potato design firmly onto the card. Experiment with two or more colors to give your pattern contrast and variety.

A. Paint a simple shape on the dried, cut-side of a potato. India ink will do very nicely.

B. This cross section shows how the angle and depth of the cut should appear.

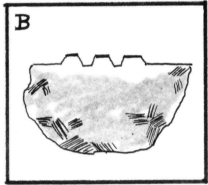

To the left are just a few of the limitless varieties of shapes that can be cut on artgum erasers. The bouquet pattern on the opposite page shows one way in which they can be effectively combined.

happy
Moms
day

Printing with an art gum or a soap eraser is basically the same as with the potato. However, their durability makes them preferable. In fact, they tend to become harder with time, thus creating a stronger printing surface.

You'll find them in a variety of sizes, ranging from 1″ x 1″ x 1″ to 3″ x 3″ x 1″. For a larger block, several can be glued together with Elmers' glue or Duco cement. I recommend an X-acto knife as a cutting tool because of its flexibility.

A. Cut base from Styrofoam cup. Then slit the side as demonstrated.

B. Flatten and weight down with a few hefty encyclopedia-type books. Be patient for several hours—like overnight.

C. Remove flattened Styrofoam and cut the design you've planned some hours before.

D. Cement shapes on a sturdy piece of cardboard, or better yet, a ¼ inch sheet of plywood. If you've included lettering in the design, be sure to glue it in position backwards.

E. Roll or brush paint onto plate, turn, and position on your printing paper. Apply gentle but firm pressure. Lift plate, remove your print and begin again.

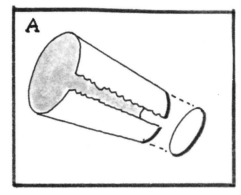

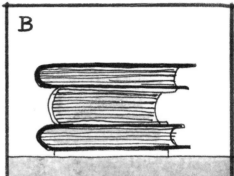

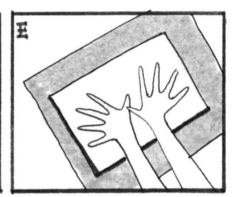

Now, let's take it a step further and create our own raised surface. Once again, there's a variety of household paraphernalia at your disposal: corrugated cardboard, ordinary pieces of cardboard, noodles which come in various widths and lengths, pieces of metal, wood, plastic and so on.

This time we need a foundation, a supporting block, on which to glue the printing shapes. Very hard, heavy cardboard or plywood are excellent. It has been my experience, though, that most cardboard tends to buckle during the washing and cleaning process. This unfortunately means the block must be weighted down each time you clean and use another color. So to avoid frazzled nerves and impatience, I recommend the plywood.

When you've collected your materials, roughly sketch your design on the block with pencil or marker. In addition to the previous printing preparations, include scissors, glue (Elmers' glue, Duco cement), and a mat or X-acto knife. An important point to remember while arranging and gluing the cut shapes is that the raised surface must be of a uniform level in order to make an even, complete print. Also allow at least 1/16" between the glued shapes to avoid clogging paint. If using a rather soft cardboard, such as the corrugated, a light coating of polymer medium, gloss or mat, before printing will help to reinforce the stamp shapes and arrest water and oil absorbency while printing. Should the design be somewhat large (over 8" x 10") and complex, I would suggest an oil-base paint to lengthen the time of application and printing. Water-base paints tend to dry out too quickly.

The actual printing can be done in two different ways:

1)   Place the printing block on the paper and apply pressure.
2)   Put the paper on the block and apply pressure with a spatula, rolling pin, a small clean brayer or simply, with the palm of your hand. Again, I would advise a test sheet to be sure the color and paint consistency is to your liking . . . then, PRINT!

One final material you might consider is Styrofoam. I've saved it for last because it can be used for various printing methods. That protective form-fitting Styrofoam from your new transistor radio, for instance, can be carefully scored to create an intaglio print (a design or figure carved or engraved below the surface). An old used-up ball-point pen or an orange-stick could be used as the scoring tools, but we'll get more involved with that later. Right now, it's those leftover washed out Styrofoam coffee cups we should be experimenting with; they're more versatile than you think.

The preparation for relief printing is quite simple. After removing the bottom with scissors or a sharp knife, cut down the side and *gently* uncurl and flatten. Placing it under a pile of books for a day or two will help eliminate the curl. Now proceed as you would with a cardboard print. Cut the desired shapes with a very sharp knife (such as an X-acto with #11 blades), then glue and mount on the foundation block. The pressure applied while printing should be gentle but firm.

This is the actual plate made by the procedure described on page 52. Once again, notice how the lettering has been cemented in reverse, in order to read correctly when finally printed.

BLOCKPRINTING

You recall at the end of the previous section, we touched on intaglio printing . . . well, this is it. The two most commonly used surfaces are linoleum blocks and soft wood. They are preferred in greeting card printing because of their simplicity, durability, and economy. Anyone can make a block print — the method of cutting and printing is quite simple, but you'll find patience to be one of the requirements too; the process takes time. However, its individuality makes it well worth the effort. A block print is made up of relatively heavy lines and solid areas in contrast to the fine hairlines obtainable in engraving or etching (pages 74 to 79). Due to its soft, pliable surface, a linoleum print will permit only the bolder, stronger lines. A woodcut, on the other hand, can range from bold to very delicate linear patterns, depending on the type of wood that is used.

Two renderings are possible: negative and positive prints. In the negative print, black areas predominate, with the art work shown mostly in white. The positive print shows the large areas in white and the art work in black line.

The negative block print is made by tooling out lines and not gouging out the large areas. The result will be similar to a chalk drawing on a blackboard. The positive block print is made in reverse, having the large areas gouged out and allowing the lines to remain in relief. The ink is then carried on the uncut surfaces and no ink is in the depressions that have been carved out.

The preliminary procedure is basically the same for both methods. Prepare your sketch as you did for the monoprint. The design doesn't have to be quite as simple as you'll have more control of the print; but since this is the first time around, it might be best to stick to a minimum of lines and shapes. Possibly an interesting anchor design for a friend going abroad via liner or maybe a stylized pumpkin on an invitation for the kids' Halloween party. In either case, your tracing, once again, should be made the same size you want the finished print. Fill in the areas that will be gouged out with a marking pen or pencil so you'll have an idea how the final print will appear.

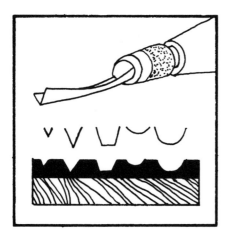

LINOLEUM BLOCK TOOLS

Shown are the various shaped linoleum blades as well as the average depth of their cut.

OK. . . now let's start with the linoleum print. Blocks can usually be purchased at the local art store mounted or unmounted, although most come mounted on a ¾" base for convenience in handling. Standard sizes range from 2" x 3" to 12" x 12". Larger sizes can be obtained through special order. One of the most attractive things about block printing is its inexpensiveness; the average price for an 8" x 10" block is about $1.75. It comes with either a dark or white surface. I recommend the latter as it can be drawn upon directly with ink or pencil. If you wish to transfer to the block by tracing, the trace lines will show up more distinctly on the white surface. Corrections are also easier to make. If, however, this is unobtainable, a thin coating of white poster-paint on the dark linoleum is almost as good. Be sure to thoroughly clean the block with soap and water before painting, since sometimes the surface is a bit oily, causing it to reject the paint.

Now, with your sketch completed and the linoleum surface prepared, here is how the design can be transferred to the block. Trace your design on the back over a light table or against a window pane. Then place your design face down on the block. Temporarily secure your design in position with cellophane tape. (Be sure that all printing reads backwards.) All lines must then be firmly penciled over again and the paper removed. Some artists insert a piece of carbon or graphite paper between the design and the block before tracing. A clear tracing should be left on the linoleum —in reverse, of course.

Your general supplies should include linoleum cutting tools, Speedball or X-acto being the most commonly used. The cutters come in either "V" or "U" shape varying from very thin for outlining to quite wide for gouging. Speedball also provides watercolor and oil inks in a wide range of colors, even fluorescent. You'll need a brayer or roller, a mixing tray or ink slab, a pile of newspapers, oil solvent if using oil inks, and some clean rags.

Papers for block printing should be absorbent for best results. While newsprint or construction paper may be used for preliminary work, the finest papers for finished work are the Oriental rice papers. The Oriental papers vary from thin as tissue to thick as blotting paper. Charcoal paper can be used but more pressure is required to overcome the grain of the paper. In any event, avoid hard-surfaced, nonabsorbent papers as they give harsh and imperfect proofs.

In cutting the paper for prints, allow at least a quarter of an inch more on all sides than the size of the block. There will thus be a surplus which can be trimmed down if necessary after the printing to make the edges parallel with the border of the design. The extra size of the paper is also needed, so that you may take hold of one of the ends of the paper protruding from the block when you pull the paper from the sticky inked surface, after it is printed.

Once you've assembled this equipment, you're ready to start cutting. TAKE YOUR TIME, and please develop the habit of carving AWAY from yourself to minimize the danger of cutting a finger or hand. The amount of pressure you place on the tool while carving will determine the depth and width of the cut. Carve lightly at first and do not try to remove too much of the linoleum at one time. Remember that you can always cut out more but you cannot replace what has already been removed.

If the linoleum seems hard or tough, hold the face of the block against a warm radiator or electric iron until the block is warm. This will facilitate the cutting.

The usual procedure in cutting is to use a small "V" shaped tool called a "veiner" to outline the design, then a larger tool to cut away the big spaces. As you cut, pushing the tool forward, be very careful to keep the depth of your cut uniform and to follow the outline exactly.

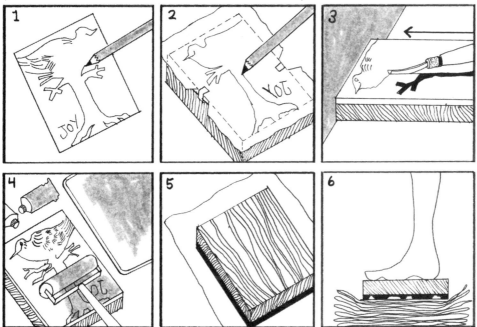

GENERAL BLOCK CUTTING AND PRINTING PROCESS

1) Make sketch to fit block size.
2) Reverse design by tracing on back of sketch and secure to block.
3) For cutting, place block against something immovable, such as a wall. Using a steady medium pressure, carefully begin to carve AWAY from yourself.
4) When the block is completed, roll on the printing ink.
5) Now cautiously lift, turn and place block on printing paper.
6) With the same care, place on newspaper and press. Remove block, carefully peel away the print and let dry.

This improvised method of block printing calls for a weathered, grainy piece of wood. Roll on the ink and print accordingly. The end results should provide a unique abstract water or sky pattern.

Another interesting block material is Styrofoam. Using a depleted ball point type pen, orange stick or similar tool, incise your design. Then follow previous printing instructions.

If your design calls for a large area to be gouged out, you should take the time to cut down to the canvas or burlap backing. Then, when the ink is applied, there's less chance of it touching this area. Next, you'll need a wide printing space. A large table protected with newspaper or a cleared floor area will do nicely. Remember, too, you'll need to have room where the prints can be laid out to dry.

The actual printing is quite simple and moves very quickly. Squeeze a healthy amount of ink onto your ink slab and roll the brayer back and forth till you hear a slight suction sound, then apply it to your block. Now, the printing can be done one of three ways. The first method, and probably the most popular, is to place your print paper on the ink block and burnish with the bowl of a tablespoon. A rolling pin or clean brayer, or even your fist may also be used. If the print paper is very thin, such as rice paper, you should place a thin piece of tracing paper over it to prevent getting excess ink that may soak through from smearing by the burnishing tool.

The second process starts by putting several newspapers on the floor. On top of this you place your printing paper and then the ink block. Now step on it carefully but firmly. Be sure to use the ball or heel of your foot to afford the most pressure. Finally, if you really get involved with block printing, you might invest in an inexpensive printing press.

Now with the experience of one-color block printing under your belt, consider multi-color printing. This process requires two or more blocks, one for each color. One is the key block which carries the dark ink and most of the detail. The trick is in making careful registration. In other words, each block should in some way be identically marked so you'll know exactly where to place it while printing. A small notch on each side or a dark pencil line will suffice. The register mark should also be lightly penciled on the printing paper before inking to key the blocks. Be sure to allow each print to dry thoroughly before adding another color. When printing one color over another, the results can be unpredictable as the amount of ink rolled on each block will vary. The watercolor inks will be more translucent than the oil inks, and so on. Part of the fun will be in experimenting with the wide variety of possibilities and perhaps coming up with an original effect of your own.

One other block material mentioned briefly in the previous chapter is Styrofoam. With an orange stick or similar object, it's possible to score a rather delicate linear pattern, such as snowflakes or feathers. Additional shapes can be created by carefully pressing objects into the Styrofoam surface. Bottle caps, a small chain, combs, jewelry, nuts and bolts are just a few of the limitless assortment of things you can try. Getting the material shouldn't prove to be a problem. Besides those flattened Styrofoam coffee cups, check out the packaging used for meats in the supermarket. Also inquire at the hardware and lumber stores. Better yet, see if the art store carries Styro-board.

Due to the soft nature of the material, I don't advise the foot pressure method of printing. Restrained burnishing will provide the best results.

Once you've gained some degree of skill and confidence, experiment with other printing materials. Instead of using paper, for instance, why not try a well ironed, absorbent fabric such as silk, fine linen or cotton! Trim the edges after printing with pinking shears or upholstery braid and carefully glue to a heavier card stock. Who knows, you could be a budding textile designer!

Or try this one. Rather than squeezing just one color on the ink slab, how about two? Place them 3 or 4 inches apart so that you'll have a color on each side of the brayer. You have to be careful not to mix the colors too much, so roll as little as possible. The results can be very effective and surprising. Incidentally, block printing lends itself beautifully to repeating in different combinations. Here a small abstract shape can be printed to use as a border, an overall pattern, or combined to form new shapes.

WOODCUT PRINTING

Wood engraving is the process of cutting into the end grain of a rather dense, harder wood. Cherry or apple woods are good. This can produce very fine, precise detail, but requires special skills and tools and is not what I'm recommending here. Rather I'm suggesting wood cutting, which is done very much in the same manner as linoleum cuts. The wood is used from the *side* grain (like any regular plank) and should be of soft pine. Since even soft wood is a harder material, you'll need high quality steel wood cutting blades. Wood can be purchased inexpensively at the local lumber yard or you can scrounge around for old weathered boards that will impart special textured effects you can take advantage of in your printing. The rest of your equipment, preparations and printing steps are simply a carry-over from the linoleum procedure.

Designed by Randall Enos

REPEAT DESIGNS

When decorative designs are used on large surfaces, such as gift wrapping papers, it is usually necessary to repeat a single design unit in some pattern over the area to be covered. You will observe these repeat patterns particularly on Christmas wrappings.

Small, simple design units are particularly desirable for the hand printing methods of block printing and silk screening. Craftsminded artists who work with these processes can easily print a small motif on wrapping paper, but find that a single design large enough to cover the entire piece of paper is too unwieldy to be practical. A repeat arrangement is the solution, using a design unit that will lend itself well to such treatment.

Using the single design unit shown in Fig. 1, let us now make several arrangements with the half-drop plan. It is best worked in vertical rows, the first unit of the second row being printed a half unit lower than the first unit of the first row (Fig. 2). When the sheet is turned 90 degrees to the right or left, they form a horizontal half-drop, which gives a feeling of motion and continuity, because the elements or units overlap like bricks in a wall, and the limits of the design unit are not apparent. We find a new half-drop arrangement in Fig. 3; here you see the unit reversed in alternate vertical rows, making an entirely new white shape in the pattern.

Two motifs have been used on the remaining patterns for design purposes. The checkerboard pattern is used and various reverse and half-drop plans have been worked out.

Try arranging your own design for repeat patterns. You will discover many other effective arrangements for realistic and abstract design.

Before laying out a gift wrap design, try to have a complete mental picture of what you want to create. Visualize the pattern so clearly that you can see it on the paper, for it is excellent training to try to see one's work in the imagination.

FIG. 1

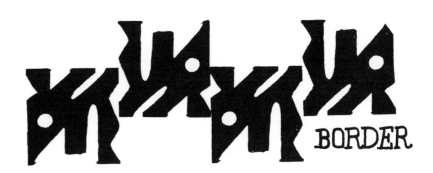

BORDER

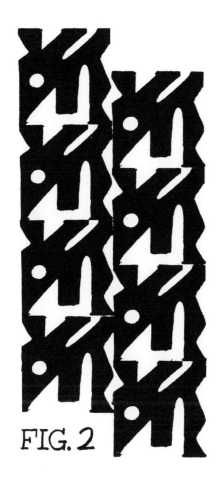

FIG. 2

FIG. 3.

BLOCK PRINTING WITHOUT BLOCKS

There is a method for producing a drawing that appears to have been cut out of linoleum but is actually done entirely with poster paint and a good waterproof India ink. The procedure is as follows:

1) Sketch out your finished design in pencil on extra heavy illustration board.

2) With a watercolor brush go over your pencil lines with a white poster paint. Add a tiny amount of light blue to the white poster paint so that it will be visible against the white paper. Be sure the paint is put on quite thick and allow to dry for several hours.

3) When your drawing is thoroughly dry, carefully brush black India ink over the entire drawing. This will cover not only the unpainted white areas of the board, but the poster color painted parts as well. Be very careful not to scrub into the poster paint with your black ink. When this has been completed, set it aside to thoroughly dry.

4) Now place your drawing under running, lukewarm water and, with cotton or a soft sable brush carefully wash away the soluble poster paint. Do this operation as quickly as possible so that the board does not become too saturated; then place your drawing between heavily weighted newspapers or magazines to dry.

It is well worth your time to experiment with this method. The drawings are barely discernible from an actual block print and many effects are possible which are very difficult to produce on an actual linoleum block.

While it is true that you can make only one print by this method, your printer can have a line engraving or offset photo made of it and any number of copies can be produced on greeting cards.

Block printing without a block. This method is easier to control than cutting either a block of linoleum or wood.

Linoleum blockprint birthday card design.
The date, incidently, being March 17, accounts
for the shamrocks.

Simplicity in composition gives this
Christmas card design individuality.
Woodcut by Grisha Dotzenko.

The charm of a New England village in winter
is beautifully expressed in this deceptively
simple-looking woodcut. Woodcut by
Grisha Dotzenko.

and It CAME TO PASS.....

STENCIL PRINTING

I'm sure you've seen various machine-cut alphabet stencils in art or stationery stores. In most cases they're used for putting the name on the mailbox or the family camping equipment or "My Tillie" on the stern of the rowboat or, more often, the "wet paint" sign on some recently renovated object. Unfortunately, the styles of lettering are limited and usually very mechanical in appearance. So, we'll simply cut our own and other shapes and patterns to fit the occasion.

Those of you who are last minute Christmas card-makers or have a minimum amount of patience will really appreciate this method. Believe me, it takes no time at all to cut a stencil and when using water-base paints, the process moves even faster. Another very attractive feature is that it requires very few, inexpensive materials. However, it's only fair to mention that the process doesn't have the longevity of block and woodcut printing because of the nature of the stencil. The fibers of even your sturdiest papers tend to become frayed after repeated printing. So for starters, I recommend a good, firm, medium to heavy-weight paper, preferably stencil paper.

This is a heavy oiled paper which will withstand rough handling. It's available in sheets (18" x 24" for about 20¢, 24" x 36" for 40¢), rolls (48" x 10 yards for $2.00), and by the yard (about $1.25 per yard). You should also consider a medium weight acetate it may prove more durable in the long run than stencil paper. If you find yourself in a real time-bind, however, and these materials aren't immediately attainable, you can resort to a piece of shirtboard. Because this is a soft fiberous material, similar to medium-weight construction paper, it won't be long before the cut edges become frayed. Still, you should be able to get two to possibly three dozen good sharp prints. Since some papers will stand up better than others, you'll have to experiment with various types and weights to compare.

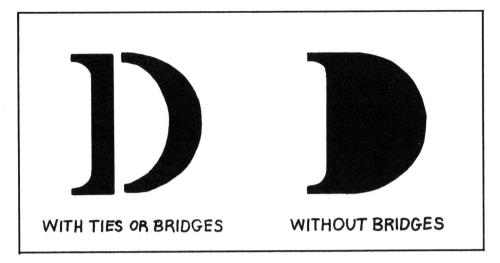

WITH TIES OR BRIDGES   WITHOUT BRIDGES

In addition to stencil paper, you'll need a sharp cutting tool (X-acto knife or razor blade), tracing paper for your sketch, printing paper (relatively absorbent medium-weight to avoid buckling). Paints are either oil or water-base or you may want to use a can of spray paint (available in a variety of colors, even fluorescent. You will also need a large water jar if using paints and naturally a palette — a dinner plate will work fine. You can buy a brush specifically designed for stencil printing. They're round with square tops and come in various sizes, like any other brush (about 50¢ for a medium size). Or try a small sponge for a more textural effect. In fact, you probably have an extra one stashed with the cleaning stuff under the kitchen sink. If you do, it's certainly worth the experiment.

Before you begin sketching your design, it's important for you to understand that stencil shapes usually require "ties" or "bridges" to make the image complete. When cutting the letter "D", for example, you would have to leave a small portion of stencil paper (a tie) between the vertical member of the "D" and the loop part. Otherwise, the center area would fall out. Note diagram.

With that in mind, let's make a sketch as you've done previously. Is your nephew graduating this June? If so, printing your best wishes will certainly make him feel very special. Or do you have a good friend who will be retiring soon? Well, why not give him the same personal treatment. The designs can be as complex as your linoleum or woodcut prints; and, incidentally, you don't have to be concerned with flopping the sketch on the stencil paper since you can do the actual printing on the same side you've traced your sketch.

Once you've transferred the design, place a piece of heavy cardboard or plywood under the stencil to protect the table surface you're cutting on. As you begin to cut, bear in mind that the areas you remove will print and those not cut out will block the color — and don't forget those ties or bridges! By the way, should these connecting pieces be accidentally cut or become worn, don't despair. They can easily be repaired with cellophane tape.

TIE-BRIDGES

In addition to making your shapes complete, the "ties" or "bridges" help to reinforce the stencil, especially when your design has many large shapes. The connecting "ties" next to the tuning knobs on the guitar aren't really necessary to attach the center bar as this has been done at the base. But they do help to keep the bar from flapping up while printing. Something to consider.

When you've completed the cutting, there are various ways to position the stencil on the printing paper. You can simply hold it with the hand not used for printing. However, it's not very practical since the odds in favor of slipping are too great. It would be best to secure the corners with tacks, masking tape or paper clips, especially when involved with two or more colors. If the stencil paper is smaller than your printing paper, be sure to protect the exposed edges with newspaper, particularly if you're using spray paint.

Now assemble your printing materials and let's get started. If you are using a sponge, wet it first, then wring it as dry as you possibly can. Any excess water could bleed under your stencil while printing and cause a ragged edge. Now dip the sponge into the desired color and dab, quickly, but carefully, around the edges to the center. Should you want to over-print with another color for a mottled effect, rinse the sponge thoroughly in your water jar and repeat the process. Allow the color to set on the card for a moment or two before lifting the stencil, then remove slowly to prevent ragged edges.

SINGLE STENCIL PRINTING

1) Sketch your design (remember those bridges).
2) Transfer sketch to stencil, and cut.
3) Position stencil on printing paper and secure. Protect exposed edges if spraying.
4) Select a printing tool and print. Be it a sponge, or,
5) spray can. Let stand a moment or two, then remove the stencil.
6) Now add desired trim and message.

The procedure is the same if using the stencil brush. Any additional detail, a bit of trim or salutation, can be done by hand once the paint has dried. However, you can also create some interesting effects by dusting *partially* dried paint with sparkle, sequins, flock, etc. I recommend oil paints as they take a little longer to dry, leaving you more time to experiment. While you're at it, why not try overprinting with the same stencil for a repeated pattern and, if there is no lettering involved, consider turning the stencil over for a reverse print — a great way to show a swinging bell for your next New Year card.

Still another possibility is printing with the shape you cut OUT of your stencil, especially if it's a simple one-piece shape like the anchor shown in the demonstration. The printing process is the same, but the results are reversed. In other words, the space around your image will be painted. A little dab of rubber cement will hold the shape in place and putting masking tape on the edges of your printing paper will leave a nice contrasting border. Going a step further and with just a little added effort, you can create an even more interesting design by combining both methods. Simply print with the cut-out shape first for a nice background color, let dry, then overprint with the stencil for your second shape. This method also gives you the opportunity of using two colors, three including the paper stock.

Now that you've become an accomplished single stencil printer, you might want to try your hand at multi-stencil printing — a separate stencil for each color. The project is naturally a little more time-consuming, but it's just as simple and I'm sure you'll find the end results well worth the experiment. Like multiblock printing, registering each stencil will be the biggest headache. It's necessary, however, for an exact duplication of your print. I have shown one approach to transferring the design and keying the stencils. If using notches as register marks, be sure to make a light pencil indication on the printing paper as you did for the linoleum blocks and naturally wait for the paint to dry between each stencil used.

REVERSE PRINTING

First print with one side of the stencil, let dry. Then turn the stencil over, position and repeat the same printing process or try another.

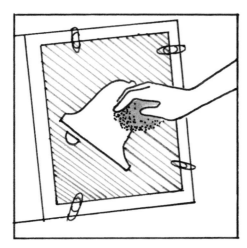

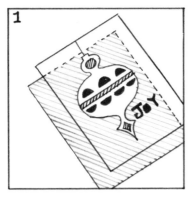
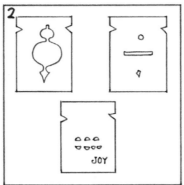
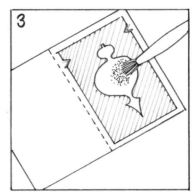

MULTI-STENCIL PRINTING

1) Make sketch on tracing paper the same size as your stencil paper.
2) Transfer the shapes that are color keyed to that stencil. In other words, all the shapes you want to be printed red should be on one stencil, and so on for greens, blues, etc.
3) If using notches to key your stencils, be sure to do the same on your printing paper (light pencil marks). Now, choose your tools and come out printing.

This method is really great should you want to create an animated effect —showing a bird on the wing, for example, with a gamey message like "We've flown the coop for Europe . . . see you in three weeks." You simply make one stencil of a bird with the wings up, another with the wings half way down, and still another with them completely lowered and so on. Overlap the bird shapes for a stronger suggestion of motion and try printing with ink, dyes or watercolor to create a transparent look.

Since a stencil is simply an object or shape that covers or masks an area from being painted, sprayed, inked, etc., you don't have to feel limited to buying or making your own. There are plenty of household and natural objects that can be creatively combined to produce some very exciting effects. Trivets, leaves, wire mesh string, combs, jewelry, washers, paper clips, or any other articles you happen to think of, even some of the found-object stamps used earlier present interesting possibilities as stencils. Then you

FOUND-OBJECT STENCILS

Arrange found objects on your printing paper. Secure with a dab of rubber cement if necessary. In this case, I recommend using spray paint or a tooth brush so as not to dislodge the objects. (But use water-soluble paint for easier cleanup.)

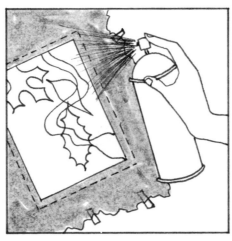

can turn around and add a stamp pattern — the textural contrast will create a highly individual design. Or see what happens when you stencil over a monoprint or blockprint. Let your imagination have a heyday . . . be curious!

Now if you've chosen the spray paint method, the printing preparations are basically the same. You may want to tack stencil and paper on a protected wall if you feel more comfortable spraying straight out in front of you rather than on a diagonal. Either way, the important thing to remember is to spray *lightly* to avoid dripping and bleeding edges. (And, follow directions about spraying in a ventilated area.) Another easy method of applying your paint is by spattering with a toothbrush. This can be done by scraping the bristles with your finger or with a small stick. The paint should have a consistency of medium cream.

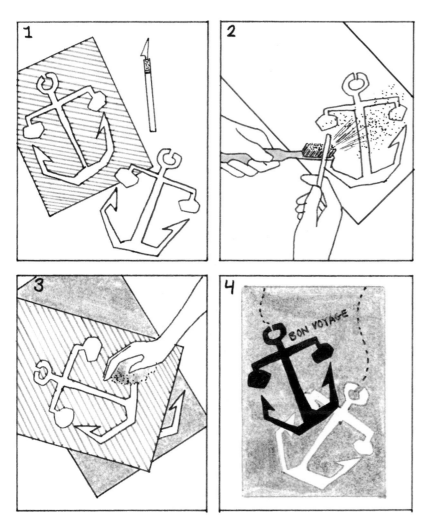

STENCIL AND TEMPLATE PRINTING

1) Make sketch, transfer to stencil paper and cut — but this time, keep the piece that has been cut out.
2) Position and secure this piece on your printing paper with a dab of rubber cement. I suggest either the toothbrush or spray paint method as you'll be covering a wide area. Let dry.
3) Now position the stencil and secure. This time why not use another method of printing for contrast.
4) When thoroughly dry, add final detail and message.

Instead of being used as a tool, this stencil cut was sent as the actual card.

PEACE

A doily and spray paint provided this lacy stencil pattern. The lettering was also done by stencil.

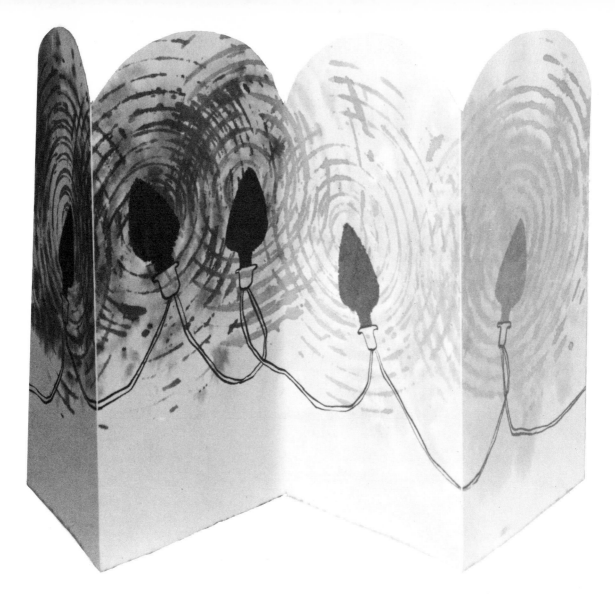

Three techniques made up this colorful design.

1. Wet-in-wet watercolor for the background — a brush used for the radiating pattern.

2. A sponge was used to apply acrylic paint to light bulb stencil.

3. Pen and ink created the holders and connecting wires.

Stenciling on already printed material such as magazine clippings, photos, newspaper, wrapping paper, etc., has unlimited possibilities.

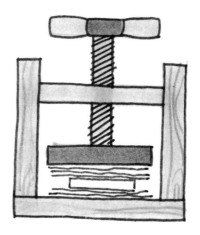

Etching

You no doubt already have most of the necessary equipment on hand from past experiments: some light to medium weight Bristol paper with a slight tooth, preferably white or in pastel colors, construction paper, X-acto knife or razor, metal-edged ruler, tracing paper and pencil for sketch, turpentine and a bunch of rags for general clean-up. In addition, you will need a piece of heavy acetate, a sharp pointed metal object to incise your design (a sturdy yarn needle secured in a dowel will do, or a peg awl from the hardware store, or a small ice pick, etc.), black etching ink, a dabber or stencil-type brush to apply the ink to the plate, a roll of paper towels and several sheets of construction or blotter paper.

The one essential piece of equipment you may not have is a press . . . a simple one. If you were lucky enough to acquire a screw press with your block printing kit, then you're all set. If this is not the case, then you can improvise very nicely with a clothes wringer. Some of the newer models have vertical clamps which can be secured on the arm or back of a heavy chair. The real old fashioned ones may have a means to be fastened to a flat wooden base with screws.

The beauty of this method of printing is that it's fast, relatively inexpensive, and creates little mess. Better yet, you are able to produce anything from a very simple to an elaborate linear pattern. It's all a matter of time and expression. If say, you've been elected to make the wedding invitation for a friend or relation, you might want to score a very intricate, delicate pattern with loads of curliques, hearts and flowers. On the other hand, a simple shamrock or shillelagh design for an impromptu Saint Patrick's Day party can be produced in no time at all with this method — easily in half a day's time.

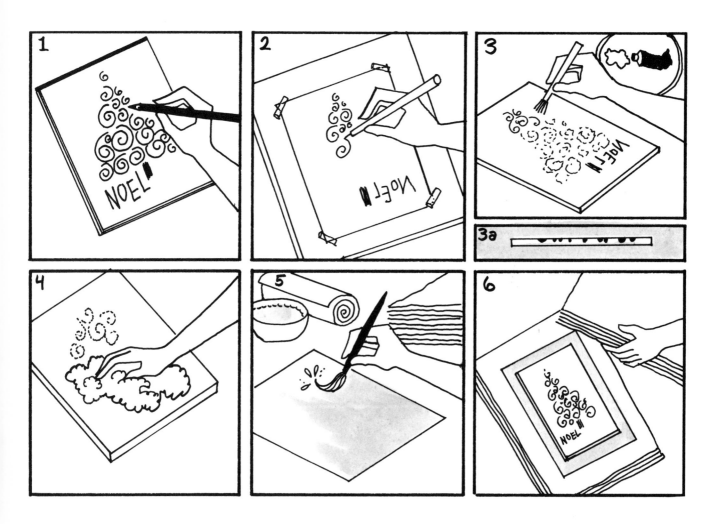

1) Make sketch on tracing paper. Also cut acetate to size.
2) Reverse sketch, attach acetate with scotch tape and score design.
3) Remove sketch and dab plate with etching ink.
3a) In profile, the inked plate will appear like this.

4) Carefully wipe off excess ink with rag.
5) Dampen printing paper with water. Stack and alternate with paper towels.
6) Place a dampened piece of printing paper on a few sheets of construction or blotter paper. Position inked plate on top, then cover with a few more sheets of construction paper to create a "sandwich."

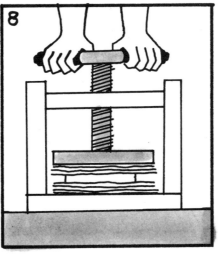

7) Carefully crank "sandwich" through wringer.
8) Or, press down hard with screw press.
9) Now, slowly remove print, re-ink plate and carry on.

So with that in mind and a completed sketch in hand, we're ready to get started. The basic steps of cutting the acetate to size, incising the design and inking should be familiar ones if you have experimented with the previously described printing methods. If not, here's a recap. I know you'll find the procedure simple as well as enjoyable.

The first stage is to cut the acetate to size by using metal ruler and an X-acto knife or razor. It should be at least 2" larger than your sketch. Be sure to flop the design before positioning the acetate, otherwise the final print will come out in reverse. Putting four small pieces of rolled scotch tape between sketch and acetate in the corners will keep them from slipping while etching. Now, with the sharp pointed tool, carefully groove or scratch out the design. Take your time! It's practically impossible to get rid of an un- wanted scratch mark. When completed, squeeze a dollop or so of printer's ink onto a small dish and dab the scored lines with stencil brush or dabber. Wipe off excess ink with a clean rag and put aside for the moment.

The next step is to cut your paper to size if you haven't already done so. It doesn't necessarily have to be cut down to the size of the eventual card, but it should at least accommodate the size of the wringer or press. Just before you begin to print, dampen the paper with a large brush and clean water. You can prepare a stack of paper by placing the sheets between alternate layers of paper towels or blotter paper. Now lay a dampened sheet of paper on a few sheets of construction paper and carefully place your inked plate face down on the paper. Then add a few more sheets of construction or blotter paper placed on top to create a "sandwich." Note instruction drawings.

The final step is to carefully feed this sandwich through the wringer, or press down hard if using a screw-type press. When released, simply remove the print, re-ink the plate and start the process all over again.

Try not to be discouraged if the first prints are not consistently dark. The width and depth of your score lines determine this. After making the first print, you may want to re-score some of the lines that appear light or possibly add a few more. The pressure of the press or wringer and dampness of the paper will also have a bearing on the sharpness of the design. Because of this flexibility, be prepared to chalk up the first few prints to trial and error.

Once you get the hang of it, there are loads of variations you can try. Rather than wiping off all the excess ink from the plate, why not leave a few areas for tone and shading. Or while dampening your print paper, consider a touch of color. A soft, pastel wet-on-wet technique would offer a nice contrast from the sharp linear pattern. Adding color or texture after the prints have dried is still another possibility.

Incidentally, if you've really taken a liking to this simplified process of etching, you may want to experiment with the more involved, professional method. Instead of an acetate plate, the drawing is scribed on a copper or zinc plate which has been coated with a thin layer of acid resisting wax. Using an etching needle, the artist scores the lines thru the wax, exposing the metal which is then etched with acid to the desired width and depth. Upon completion, the plate is then inked and reproductions are made on an etching press. It sounds complicated, and there are other variations such as dry-point, engraving, etc., but actually it's just as simple as our abbreviated method, only more time-consuming.

As suggested in previous chapters, should this be your first stab at professional etching, I recommend investing in a kit that will completely outfit you with all the necessary equipment and instructions. Weber puts out a very complete kit which includes a copper plate, yellow transfer paper, a ball of hard etching ground, one 2½ oz. bottle each of stopping-out varnish and plate oil, rubber roller, etching needle and scraper, burnisher, wax tapers, polishing powder, ink dabber, brushes, emery paper, oil stone, three tubes of etching ink, and most important, a hand vise.

Designed by Gabor Peterdi

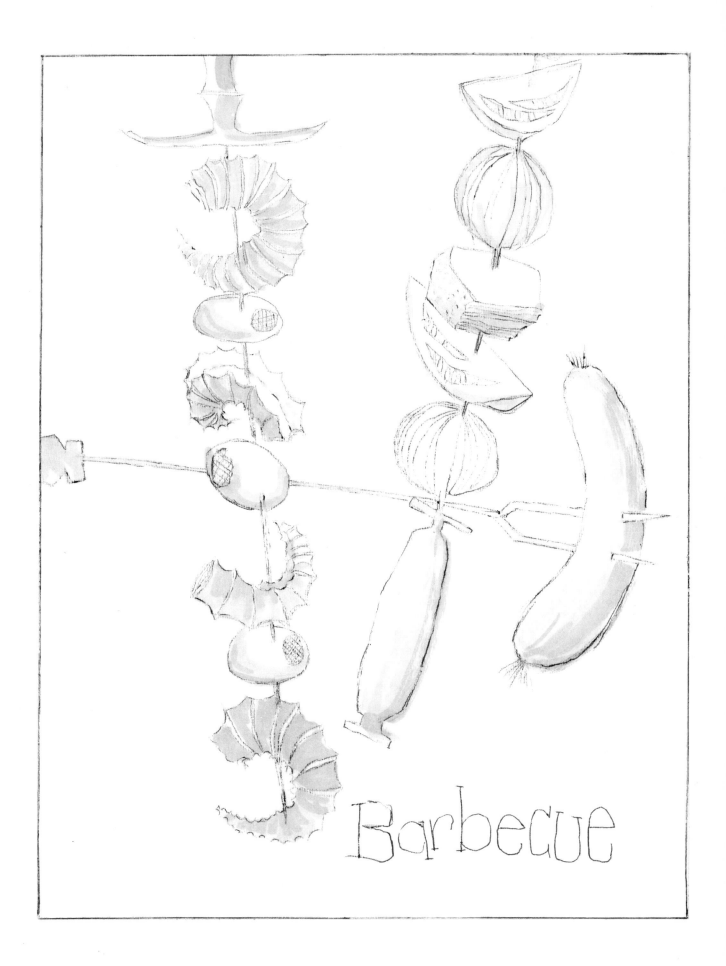

Barbecue

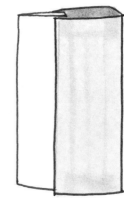

SILKSCREEN PRINTING

With the experience of stencil printing under your belt, it would be only natural to want to try a more advanced method—silk screening. This fascinating and rapidly expanding method of printing owes its origin to the Chinese who, some 1,500 years ago, used it for decorating pottery. A design cut from parchment was held in place within a wooden frame by fine silk threads. The article to be decorated was then placed beneath the screen and ink applied, which penetrated the open areas of the mesh, leaving on the article a replica of the design.

Although today's equipment is much improved, the printing process is basically the same. Paints or inks are easily forced through the meshes of a silk, nylon or cotton organdy screen to print images on the card. The device used to draw the paint across the screen is called a squeegee and can be simply described as a sturdy flat piece of rubber mounted in a piece of wood which serves as a handle.

These are your basic tools: paint or ink, a mounted silk screen and a squeegee. In addition, you will need lacquer, lacquer filler and thinner, transparent base, block-out dope and applicator, water soluble film, stencil cutting knife, masking tape and a stirring stick. If this is your first attempt at silk screening, it might be easiest to invest in an inexpensive silk screen set. These contain most of the previously listed materials and sell for about $15 to $20, complete with instructions. They provide the means for training in color mixing, squeegee application and the absolutely essential off-contact printing technique that assures clean, crisp images.

Naturally, the size of the screen, the amount of paint or ink and stencil film will determine the price. The screen comes already stretched on the frame and hinged to a smooth base. One thing you should always keep in mind is that the printing area of the screen will be at least 2 inches less than the frame size. In other words, if you've ordered a 10"x13" frame, only 8"x11" of the screen is usable printing space. Actually it will be even less when you've masked the edges of the frame to prevent the paint from seeping between frame and screen. After this protective measure, the final design area will be about 6"x 9".

Designed by George Zariff

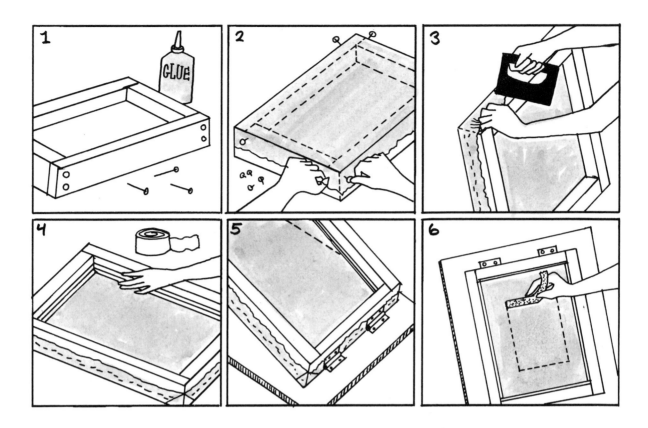

But if you feel ambitious enough to make your own frame, the construction isn't as difficult as it may seem. Remember, you should plan the inside dimensions to be about 4" wider and 6" longer than the design to be printed. This will provide a reservoir area for the paint. I suggest Weldwood or Elmer's glue and nails to secure the corners of the frame. Attaching the silk to the frame is a little trickier and requires more patience. Cut the silk 2" larger all around than the frame and tack 3 corners loosely with push pins or thumb tacks. Now stretch the fourth corner and permanently fasten with tacks or staple gun. (I prefer the latter.) From this point, slowly and carefully stretch and secure the adjacent two sides, continue around until you've completed the frame. If using tacks, be sure they're flush with the wood. In the event you happen to be the type of person who goes about making things in a big way, an extra pair of hands can be very helpful to tack while you stretch or vice-versa.

The next step is to prepare the corners and edges inside the screen to avoid paint seepage. For this you cut four 1½"x 2" strips of paper an inch longer than the length and width of the inside frame, this will afford a ½" overlap at each corner. Moisten strips with ordinary casein glue thinned with half as much water and place around inside the frame. When dry, apply 2 coats of shellac to paper, being careful not to splatter on screen. A still simpler method is to use gummed brown paper tape which you can pick up next time you're in the stationery store. Cut the appropriate lengths, dampen the gummed area with sponge and adhere. Nothin' to it. The base for the screen, where your printing paper will be placed, should be about two or three inches larger than the frame — ¼ inch plywood will do very nicely. While you're at the lumber store, purchase two loose-pin hinges to fasten frame to base — the pins should be easily removable to facilitate cleaning and lacquering.

FRAME CONSTRUCTION, SCREEN PREPARATION AND GENERAL PRINTING PROCEDURE

1) Glue and nail wood frame together.

2) Carefully stretch silk.

3) Tack or staple screen.

4) Cut gum tape to size. Apply to *inside* corners and sides of frame.

5) Connect frame and base with two loose-pin hinges. Be sure the screen is flush with the base.

6) Now using masking or cellophane tape, frame the printing area.

7) Remove screen from base and mount on blocks.

8) Place art work in position. Brush on fill-in lacquer and let dry. Turn screen over and brush lacquer on the other side. Remove tape when lacquer is dry and repace screen.

9) Another block-out procedure is to tape newspaper or kraft paper in place of the fill-in lacquer.

10) Lift screen and use small strips of masking tape to make the registry guides on the baseboard. (This facilitates the positioning of your card paper.) Put card stock in place.

11) Lower screen and squeeze paint on upper protected part of the screen. Then draw squeegie toward you with medium pressure.

12) Lift screen carefully, remove print and either lay on flat surface or hang on clothes line device to dry.

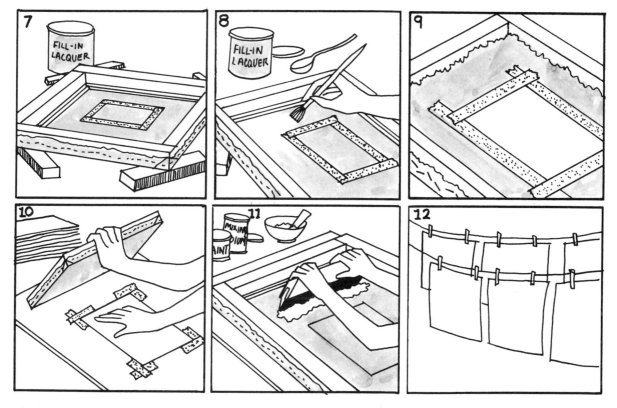

This being one of the most popular forms of home and commercial printing, your local art store probably carries the essential paint and inks used for silk screening. Special oil-type paints and lacquers are available on the market and are particularly formulated for silk screen work. Tempera colors, however, are also excellent for printing and have the advantage of easy handling and cleaning. Their being opaque makes it possible to overprint in many colors. Manufacturers have developed a mixing medium to facilitate silk screen printing with tempera. When one part of this mixing medium is added to one part tempera color, a perfect silk screen ink is produced. This medium is obtainable at any art supply store. Your mixture should be just thick enough so that it does not drip off the edge of the squeegee. If it is too thin, your printed image will not be even in tone and sharp at the edges.

Now that you're armed with frame, squeegee, choice of colors, etc., let's consider the three basic silk screen methods:

THE STENCIL SCREEN METHOD

This consists of cutting a stencil and adhering it to the screen. Then the unused area around the stencil is filled in with block out lacquer or tape. The paper is positioned under the screen. A squeegee is then pulled across the screen forcing ink through the open mesh of the silk to the paper beneath.

THE GLUE METHOD

With this method you paint directly on silk with glue, covering all areas you do not wish to be printed. A water-soluble fish-type glue, which can be thinned with water to the right consistency is best. Serigraphs are prepared in this manner, using the transparent base. This is probably the simplest method to use, except where fine line is required.

THE TUSCHE AND GLUE METHOD

This approach may be used when you want to make a positive drawing directly on the silk. You paint the design on the silk with tusche; then cover the entire surface with glue. Next, the tusche is removed from the printing area of the screen by scrubbing from the back with turpentine and a soft rag.

THE PHOTO FILM METHOD

A more complete description of this procedure will follow in the next section on photo printing.

While contemplating which process to try and what to print, let's set up your printing area. Choose a fairly well-ventilated room to dissipate the lacquer and paint odors. You'll need a large table protected with newspapers on which to place the silk screen frame, loads of paper towels and rags for cleaning up. Add to these four small pieces of scrap wood of equal size to elevate the screen for cleaning and lacquering (note diagram). Choice of print paper will be no problem, as most of the paper stocks described in Chapter 2 will be suitable. In fact, why not have a variety on hand: newsprint, construction, a few laminated or metallic paper stocks, or maybe some leftover rice paper from your block-printing days? The contrast in surface texture will have an interesting if not surprising effect on your print, possibly more desirable than your original intentions. I hope you've been thinking up an idea while arranging your equipment. If you have and been successful, how about a sketch? However, if nothing inspiring comes to mind, take advantage of the idea files. Remember what was mentioned about the size of the frame in relation to your actual printing area.

Should you want to print a background color, this must be done before adding stencil or glue. Once again, if this is your first attempt at silk screening, it's a great way to become familiar with the handling and proper pressure of the squeegee, the amount of paint used while printing and its consistency.

Now hinge the screen frame back on its base. Insert a plain sheet of paper and lower the frame. Pour a small quantity of paint on the silk along one edge of the screen. Pull the squeegee over the paint and toward you in one smooth, firm motion. Remove the paper and check for any imperfections in the screening. Now you are ready to print the cards by inserting them one by one. After removing each printed card, lay it on a flat surface. Do not let them touch or they will smudge. After you have done about 30 cards, carefully place a sheet of newspaper over them and begin a second layer. You can screen as many colors as you like, one after the other, as long as the cards are not piled directly on top of each other after being printed. Allow the cards to dry for about 24 hours.

Cleaning the screen is relatively easy. Insert a piece of newspaper under the empty frame. Discard excess paint with a piece of cardboard or spatula. Then remove the frame from its base. Place the frame on a protected surface and remove all the paint with turpentine.

If you plan to repeat use of the same design, the glue size does not have to be removed, but the paint should always be thoroughly removed from the screen immediately after printing each color. When you are finally finished with the design itself, simply rinse out the glue with hot water until the screen is quite clean. It then can be used repeatedly in the same way, for other designs.

If you've decided on the stencil screen method, the steps are also very simple. First, tape your original card design to the work surface. The lacquer stencil film is covered with transparent paper on one side and is orange on the other side. Tape the stencil film over the card with the orange side up.

STENCIL SILK SCREEN METHOD

1) Make sketch. Then place stencil film over sketch and secure. Be sure orange side is up. Using light but firm hand, cut through orange lacquer film with stencil knife. Peel away the area to be printed.

2) Raise screen, position stencil film on base, then lower screen. Once again with a light touch, apply the adhering liquid using a rubbing motion. Quickly wipe excess with a dry cloth. Slight cloudiness indicates adhering action. Once the film is firmly attached, lift frame and carefully remove the backing sheet.

3) Follow previous instructions for fill-in lacquer.

4) Position the card paper and proceed to print.

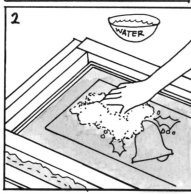

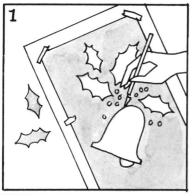

With a sharp stencil knife and a light but firm hand, cut through the lacquer film in the area to be printed white. Be careful not to cut the wax transparent backing paper on the stencil film. Peel cut film away from the backing. The stencil film is now ready for adhering. Raise the frame of the silk screen and push the card against the registry guides on the baseboard. Tape the card into position, then tape the first stencil film on top of the card. Be sure to check that the design is in place and that the triangles on the film match the ones on the card. Drop the frame.

Take two small folded pieces of cloth; wet one with adhering liquid and run it over the silk and film in small areas; using a rubbing motion, quickly go over the wet area with the dry cloth. The process of adhering is actually melting the film into the silk. It is necessary to use a light touch, otherwise the film may melt completely. If you are proceeding correctly, you will notice a slight cloudiness as the film adheres to the silk. After the stencil film has adhered, put a ruler underneath the tape to pull it up, and lift the frame. Next, remove backing sheet from the film, a little at a time. If some of the film starts to come off, adhere that spot again, making sure a piece of backing paper is behind it.

To apply the fill-in lacquer, unhinge the frame from its baseboard. Using a piece of cardboard, spread a thin coat of fill-in lacquer on the silk around the cut-out design. This is done so the paint will go only through the cut-out design. Allow this to dry, replace the frame and you're ready to paint.

If you happen to be in a real rush, however, there is a simpler version of this method. Instead of using the stencil lacquer film, dig up a couple of old shopping bags, preferably a bit lighter than supermarket weight. Kraft paper would be ideal. Trace your sketch onto this paper and cut the shapes. Lift the frame and position a trial piece of paper the same size as your card shape. The beauty of this procedure is that you have the choice of printing the positive or negative shapes. For example, should you want the space around the cut shapes to be printed, simply arrange these elements on the trial paper to duplicate the image of your sketch, then mask the area around the card shape with your fill-in lacquer as you did before. On the other hand, if you want the cutout area to be printed, simply discard the cut chapes and position the remaining paper over the trial sheet. You'll have to do a little guessing with its placement since you can't see the edges of the trial paper beneath your bag paper, but you can usually come very close to the original composition by feeling your way. In the event you were able to leave a lot of bag area around the cut shapes, say a good 5" to 6", great! it won't be necessary to use the fill-in lacquer. Once either method has been arranged to your satisfaction, carefully lower the frame. Now dab some paint on the edge of the screen that's farthest from you and follow the sqeegee instructions discribed earlier in the chapter. A single coating will act as an adherent to your stencil. Lift the frame gingerly, replace the trial paper with the card paper and carry on. This is not, I'm afraid, a reliable method for longevity and 100% sharp, crisp prints, but it will suffice if you've decided on an impromtu party.

Incidentally, you might try experimenting with some ready made stencils. Nature, for example, has an abundance of contrasting shapes to choose from: leaves, grass blades, ferns, flowers, feathers, etc. Also consider various man-made sundries such as doilies or ribbons to get you started.

Still another thought is to place a piece of loose weave material between the screen and your printing paper for an interesting textural effect.

In fact, why not try this with the next silk screen process: the glue method?

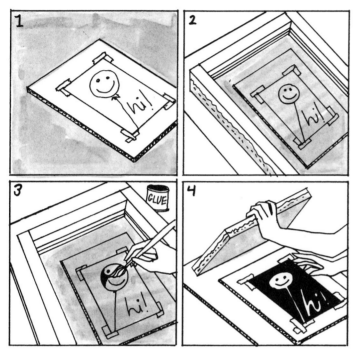

GLUE SILKSCREEN METHOD

1) Sketch design and place on cardboard.

2) Position sketch and cardboard under screen.

3) Trace design with small brush dipped in glue. Also block out area around card paper with lacquer. The space not touched with glue and lacquer will print.

4) Let dry throughly before following previous printing instructions.

First sketch out your design on a sheet of paper the size of your greeting card and place it on cardboard. Close the screen over your design and adjust the paper until your design is centered. Place register marks on cardboard so you can line up the corners or the sides of your succeeding paper or blank cards.

With your design now under the screen, trace the design with a small brush dipped in liquid glue. Add a few drops of tempera paint to the glue so you can see it better on the silk screen. The outside edge, and any pattern will not seep through. In this printing, the color will print in the areas you have not covered with glue, usually the background. Allow the glue to dry thoroughly before starting to print.

Cleanup will require a lacquer thinner after the paint has been first removed with turpentine in order to dissolve the lacquer size. Place some sheets of newspaper under the stencil film and pour a small quantity of lacquer thinner over it. Rub with fingers until the film starts to dissolve into the newspaper. Repeat this step until the screen is quite clean. Then take two clean rags saturated with thinner and rub from both sides of the screen at the same time until the silk is thoroughly clean. It is not necessary to remove all the fill-in lacquer as it can be used in the next screening. But the paint should always be thoroughly removed from the screen after use.

The tusche and glue method is also a very popular form of printing and the general procedure is the same as the glue method. The tusche allows for a bit more accuracy, however, and goes as follows:

In this process, you paint a design upon the silk screen with tusche, a very heavy paint, then cover the entire screen with glue or the "resist" as it is sometimes called. The tusche is removed from the screen by washing with turpentine or kerosene, resulting in open spaces for printing. The glue stops color from passing through the screen to the background. This method is adequate for a casual effect, and is a natural for the freehand artist since applying tusche is like painting a picture.

Lay cardboard beneath the screen to keep the wood panel clean. Draw your design on a sheet of paper the size of your greeting card and place it on the cardboard. Close screen over and adjust paper until design is centered. Now, place register marks on cardboard so you can line up the corners or sides of each succeeding card or paper.

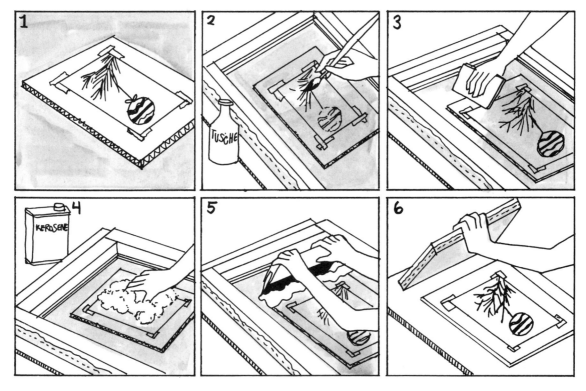

GLUE AND TUSCHE SILKSCREEN METHOD

1)   Once again, place sketch on a piece of cardboard and position under screen.

2)   Trace design with tusche. Allow to dry at least for 30 minutes.

3)   Now spread diluted warm glue over all areas you don't want printed. Cover the entire surface including the tusche. Remove excess and let dry (about 30 minutes). Apply a thin second coat and allow a good hour for drying.

4)   Next, scrub and remove glue-covered tusche with turpentine or kerosene soaked cloth.

5)   Wipe clean with dry cloth and start printing.

6)   Remove print and allow to dry as done previously.

Apply tusche directly upon the screen; keep design in position beneath the screen to trace over. Brush tusche on pattern to be printed with a small brush. Practice on paper to get the feel of the amount of tusche wanted on the brush. Though the tusche is so heavy it scarcely hardens, brace the frame open and allow to remain in this position for 30 minutes so the tusche will set. While frame is still open apply the warmed glue, diluted about one half with water, to all areas you don't want printed.

Scrape the glue evenly across the entire surface of the screen, including the parts done with tusche, with the straight edge of a cardboard. Make sure the screen is completely covered; scrape off the excess. Allow about a half hour to dry; apply a thin second coat and let dry for an hour.

Remove glue-covered tusche by scrubbing screen briskly with cloth soaked in turpentine, kerosene, or a recommended solvent. Use care when you are working with inflammable solutions. Wipe the entire screen clean with a dry cloth, revealing the open design surrounded by a solid glue area.

Important: opaque watercolors or tempera paints must not be used with any silk screen method which uses a glue as a "resist." The water in such paints will affect the glue.
Watercolor paints may only be used with the stencil screen method which employs lacquer as a size.

Designed by James Daugherty

Don't despair if first attempts do not reach the standard expected, for with this unique medium it is possible to overpaint, which in many instances improves the surface texture, so that early failures may eventually become successful.

One final experiment to consider the next time you're making a frame is to try improvising with the screen itself. Instead of the traditional flat silk, why not a textured one? An old intricately patterned silk stocking could be carefully stretched on a small frame to create a very exciting background design. Lightly brush all tack or staple holes with nail polish to prevent runs. You might print with a simple Victorian oval-shaped stencil, let dry, then hand print a Valentine or Anniversary sentiment in the center.

The variety of combinations are endless when the process gets rolling. And, don't hesitate to incorporate some printing methods from previous chapters into your experiments, together with a bit of trim, or an unusual background pattern.

Designed by Linda Powell   Courtesy, Looart Press, Inc.

This series of shapes surprinted over successively lighter shapes creates an effective impression of depth.

Another variation on the found object stencil method: a collection of assorted ferns and leaves created this impromptu design. Unfortunately, due to their fragility, you're limited to a half dozen good prints.

Used by permission of the publisher, The Printery House of Conception Abbey, Conception, Mo.

Design by Chantal.

how GOOD this world is

because of PEOPLE like you

PHOTO PRINTING

In the previous chapter we experimented with the three basic silkscreen methods using paint and ink. Now before you put screen and equipment away, consider the photo film method. It's simple, inexpensive and the results are unlike any we've produced yet. Even better is the fact that you don't need a camera, darkroom or cumbersome, costly photo equipment. Everything can be done in the same room, on the same table you've been using; just a few additional materials will be needed.

Briefly described, these photographic stencils are made by exposing your art work to a light sensitive film. The artwork or lettering should, of course, be done on a transparent positive; black opaque ink on a handy piece of transparent acetate will do very nicely. Or if you have a favorite photograph you've been saving for just the right occasion, this would be an ideal way to reproduce a whole batch of very individual cards. You just have the local photoengraver or lithographer make a transparent film positive from the photo. Consult the yellow pages or your local printer. Incidentally, you can make your own positive photographically by exposing your artwork on Eastman Auto-positive film. The artwork does not have to be transparent, since you expose through the film with a Number 2 photoflood bulb. When the auto-positive film is developed (follow accompanying instructions), you have a transparent positive, ready to be made into your photographic screen stencil.

Preparing the stencil is no more difficult than making the positive transparency. As suggested in the previous chapter, if you are very new at this, seriously consider purchasing a small introductory kit. It will be inexpensive and contain most of what you need: a couple of 10" x 12" sheets of film plus all the accessories and instructions. Craftint puts out a basic one for about $4-$5 or if unavailable locally, you can order it thru an art supply store. However, if you want to make the stencil from scratch, the basic materials you'll need are as follows: Photo stencil film, Nu-Film Eze Photo, (about $3 for a 30" x 36" sheet), sensitizer powder (makes about one pint for 65¢), adherent solvent (about $1.15 a quart or $3.00 per gallon), two trays, one for cold water and another for warm water, large enough to develop and wash the photographic stencil, a contact frame for making the exposure of transparent negative and film. An 11" x 14" frame will cost you about $11, or placing a clear piece of glass over the film and negative on a ¼" to ½" thick piece of foam rubber will suffice. And finally, a Number 2 flood lamp.

Or, with a spare socket and cord, you can devise a very workable equivalent. Simply take a piece of heavy-duty aluminum foil and carefully bunch one of the long sides until you have an umbrella or cup shape. Now attach to the upper part of the socket with string or tape to provide a reflector shield. After inserting a Number 2 photoflood bulb, suspend the socket to hang about 12" over contact frame.

Once you've assembled these materials, prepare the sensitizer as directed. Tape the silk screen film, with the emulsion side up, to a piece of cardboard with Scotch tape. The sensitizer is applied with a very soft brush; first brushed lengthwise, then crosswise. With a piece of sturdy paper or cardboard, vigorously fan the sensitized film for about 15 minutes or until dry, then remove from support by cutting the tape with a sharp knife.

Transferring the positive transparency to the film takes even less time. Simply position the film in the contact frame with the backing sheet facing you. On top of this, place the transparency, reading in reverse. Now position the frame beneath the floodlight (remember, about 12" away) and expose film and transparency for approximately 3 minutes. Those portions exposed to the light will become insoluble in water and harden. Remove the film and develop in a pan of warm water. Don't panic if you don't see the artwork immediately; it takes a few seconds for the shapes to materialize. The final step is to adhere the film to the silk screen, let dry, and carefully peel away the backing sheet. After the edges around the film have been filled in, proceed with the printing method described in the previous chapter.

Still another process of silk screen printing eliminates the photo-stencil film. This relatively new product is called Azocol and the credit goes to Colonial Process Supply Co., Inc. (note index for complete address). The package contains a bottle each of emulsion, sensitizer, and blue dye, all of which when proportionately mixed are applied directly to the silkscreen. Once dry, your film or acetate art is placed over the screen and exposed. Developing or washing out the areas not hardened by the exposure is done conveniently with warm water. Now you're ready to print. Easy.

There are two types of Azocol Direct Emulsion:
> Azocol R should be used with oil colors, synthetics, lacquers and vinyl inks.
> Azocol T works best with water soluble inks, such as pigment emulsions of the water-in-oil or oil-in-water type used in textile printing. Such screens, however, will still have to be reinforced with blockout solutions or resist coating.

PHOTO SILKSCREEN METHOD

1) Cut film about 2" larger than the positive. With emulsion side up, tape all four sides of film to piece of cardboard with masking tape. Now, using a 2" to 3" wide brush, sensitize the film first one direction, then the other. Brush lightly so that no excess sensitizer remains on the film. The final sensitizing step is to dry with electric hair dryer. (Although sensitizing may be done in the light, drying should take place at night.)

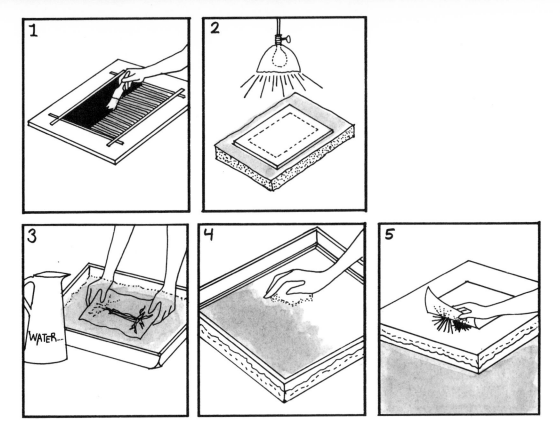

2) To expose the film, remove from cardboard and place in a contact
frame emulsion side down. Now place the positive emulsion side down
on top of film and close contact frame. Expose with No. 2 floodlight at
a distance of 20" for about two minutes. If using an arc lamp, exposure
time will be approximately 30 seconds. Time yourself carefully;
precise exposure time and good contact are essential. Overexposure
will harden the emulsion so that the film will not adhere to the silk.
Underexposure simply results in a weak stencil.

3) Third and final stage is to submerge film, after exposure, emulsion
side up, in tray or bucket. Or hose down with warm water (110°F.).
Image should appear in a few minutes. Rinse with cold water when
etching looks complete.

4) Before adhering film to screen, be sure the screen is absolutely clean.
A good detergent and plenty of hot water to remove the detergent can
be used to clean a silk screen. For a nylon screen, you can use a
10% solution of cresylic acid (Metacresol) or a 20% solution of caustic
soda (using medium-hard nylon brush). Now remove the film from the
water and lay it emulsion side up on a few pieces of newspaper.
This helps to absorb excess water. Place screen on top of film in
desired position. Then use newspaper to blot screen on the inside with
the flat of your hand. Continue this procedure until all
moisture has been removed.

5) When the screen is completely dried at room temperature or with a fan,
the backing will peel off very easily. Begin to lift the plastic
backing sheet on one corner and strip off the entire backing. Block
out and touch up with Flexiglue or an equivalent. Now the
screen is ready for printing. To remove stencil, soak screen in hot water.
Then run water over screen to eliminate any stubborn pieces of stencil. Wash
and rinse screen with detergent so that screen will be ready for future work.

BASIC PRINTING INSTRUCTIONS

1) This is the general layout of the darkroom.
   Should you be lefthanded, you may work more comfortably with a
   reverse arrangement. Keep photo paper (always in protective envelope)
   and printing objects handy on the opposite side of the "printing area."

2) When ready to print, shut off all lights except the red bulb.
   Arrange objects on glass slab. When satisfied, carefully lift glass
   and slip a sheet of photo paper beneath.

3) Now expose photo paper with white light . . . just for a second or two
   (red light may remain on at all times).

4) Remove photo paper and place in developer solution until image appears.
   Now, move quickly to the second tray of acid and water for a few
   seconds, then finally into the Hypo solution for at least 30 minutes.
   After several minutes, it's possible to turn on the white light
   (be sure the unexposed photo paper is well concealed in envelope).

5) Remove print from hypo solution and place in clean water for, again,
   about half an hour.

6) Finally, place the print on a clean tray or glass slab, sponge off
   excess water, then put on flat surface to dry; or:

7) Instead of the glass or tray surface, sponge photos on a free
   bathroom wall.

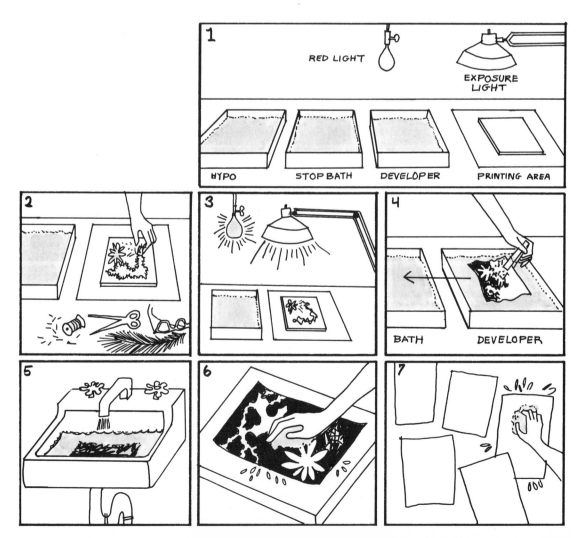

A simple arrangement of found objects: a wooden necklace, nails and string, created this interesting contact print. The size and solidity of your objects will determine their clarity.

The various steps necessary to print photographically are no more complicated than silkscreen printing. The tools and process are different, of course, but you don't have to be a shutterbug enthusiast to master them. Essentially you'll need a makeshift darkroom, an area where light can be shut out completely. If this is impossible during daylight hours, as it is in my small studio, simply wait until dark and hang "Death to all who enter" signs on the doors. To see what you are doing, however, and not expose the printing paper, you'll need a red light bulb. Or, you can improvise by painting a plain one or putting a piece of red cellophane or tissue paper over a flashlight. The next step calls for a trip to the local photo shop or large department store to pick up a pack of photo print paper, photo developer, photo fixer or hypo and acetic acid. In addition to the two trays used for developing the silk screen photo stencil, include a third one for rinsing; glass, enamel or plastic (in that order) for the best results. You'll also need a large container of water (to hold a couple of gallons) or if you happen to have a nearby sink with running water, better yet. A sponge, X-acto knife, a glass, plastic or enamel poker (about the size of a straw) to keep the photo paper submerged in the chemical solutions, a smooth, clean, flat plate or tray for sponging off excess water from the finished print and a glass slab to place over the print paper during exposure time will complete the basic list.

Fortunately, everything but the printing can be done in the daylight, which will leave your evening hours free for the fun part. Take your time setting up the darkroom and preparing the chemicals; read the directions carefully. Place the trays next to one another on a large protected table. Be sure the photo paper is well sealed (the black envelope inside the yellow carton should only be opened when the red light is on). You'll also need a strong regular light to expose the photo paper, a set up identical to the photo silk screen film and transparency procedure would be great. All the other materials should be placed within comfortable reach.

Now you can spend the rest of the day deciding what kind of photo print to make. For starters, let's try the simplest: the shadowgraph print or photogram. It requires no camera; you design the shapes and composition by arranging various found objects on the photo print paper. Take advantage of some of the articles used in our chapter on stamp printing: some string, paper clips, keys, lace, pieces of wire mesh, noodles, coins, transparent objects (like a glass figurine or apothecary top), negatives from old photographs, cut-out letters from magazines to create words and so on. And don't forget to collect from nature as well. When you've selected the objects that most appeal to you, arrange them on the glass slab that will lay over the printing paper. Now you're ready to print whenever possible.

Under the protection of the red light, take out a piece of photo paper and carefully slip it, glossy side up, beneath the glass slab with the found object. Be sure to lift the glass just slightly so as not to dislodge the arrangement, and don't forget to close the photo paper envelope. Now turn on the white light for a second or two; keep in mind that the longer you expose the photopaper the darker it will become when developed. The first few prints will be a process of trial and error, which is to be expected, so don't become too discouraged if they're not all winners.

After the exposure, remove the photopaper (under the red light) and place it first in the developer solution. Use the poker to keep the paper submerged until the shapes become clear and dark enough to suit your fancy. Next, quickly put the print into the second tray (water and acid) to stop the developing action, and then into the hypo solution to completely fix the printing process. After several minutes, it's possible to turn on the white light, but leave the sheet in the hypo solution for at least 30 minutes. The final step is to rinse the print thoroughly in the clean water for about half an hour, remove, and place on the smooth clean glass plate or a tray. Now sponge off excess water and allow to dry.

As these steps become more familiar, you'll begin to experiment with different time exposures and discover new gimmicks to help control tone and the sharpness of the shapes. Fanning your hand over certain areas of the print paper during the exposure time, for instance, will keep those portions much lighter than the others, by blocking the direct light. Or do half the exposure with the large white light, then swirl a small pen light around for the second half. Varying the height of the penlight will determine the sharpness of the linear pattern. Differing the placement of the found objects or changing them altogether during the exposure time also has exciting possibilities. The variations are endless and each one becomes more addictable than the last. In fact, because it's so easy to lose track of time while printing, it might be wise to have an alarm clock on hand, so you can let the family know you're still alive.

An interesting alternative to the shadowgraph method is to replace the found objects with a photo-etching. This is a very simple process of scratching a pattern on a clear piece of acetate and then rubbing printer's ink into the lines. The excess is removed with a cloth, leaving ink only in the black lines. If clear acetate or celluloid is not available, an old negative from which the emulsion has been removed with hot water will do.

To make a negative, first draw the design on a piece of paper. Then tape or thumbtack the film over it for easy tracing. Use a sharp-pointed instrument for a stylus, such as a sewing-machine needle, which can be held in a dowel or an automatic pencil. Innumerable effects can be

These terrific baroque masks were cut from an old discarded antique book, glued over a simple line drawing and Xeroxed. Magic Marker color was added for the final touches.

had by arranging the lines in various ways. Make a print on glossy paper and mount the finished picture on a colored card or neat folder.

Now going off into an entirely different direction in photo printing, let's take a closer look at the Xerox machine usually found in local schools, offices, libraries and stationery stores. These photocopying machines provide the simpliest, most expedient method of printing yet. If the occasion calls for many cards, you could reduce the cost by dividing the sketch paper into two or even four designs, keeping the motif the same or making each one different. I would avoid using a pattern that calls for subtle shading or large areas of solid blacks. Strong contrasting lines, outlined shapes and lettering will reproduce more successfully. Felt marker color, extra decorative detail and shading, a bit of trim, etc., can be added after the prints have been completed. You might even overprint with another printing method, hand stamps or a simple stencil, to make the card unique. For example, why not Xerox a delicate line drawing of a Christmas tree, just the tree. Then use a simply cut stamp or stencil to create the ornaments. After all the finishing touches, cut and mount the designs on colored paper. Include an inside message if desired.

Before winding up, there is still one other photo copying method you should try. Next time, instead of using the Xerox machine, consider blueprinting your designs. It's basically in the same price range and will create quite a different effect. If possible, the drawing should be done on semi-transparent paper: typewriter paper, tracing paper, vellum, or such. It will save the expense of having a transparent positive made. Just think of the reaction of your friends when they receive your blueprint announcement of moving or opening a new business. They'll be delighted and equally impressed.

If this has been your first introduction to photoprinting and you are determined to continue, great. There are many variations, some more involved and complex than others, some effects more exciting than others. The methods described in this chapter are about the simplest and least expensive. So if you've found yourself more interested in photoprinting than you thought and wish to carry it further, check out more advanced information in the library or photo store — and carry on.

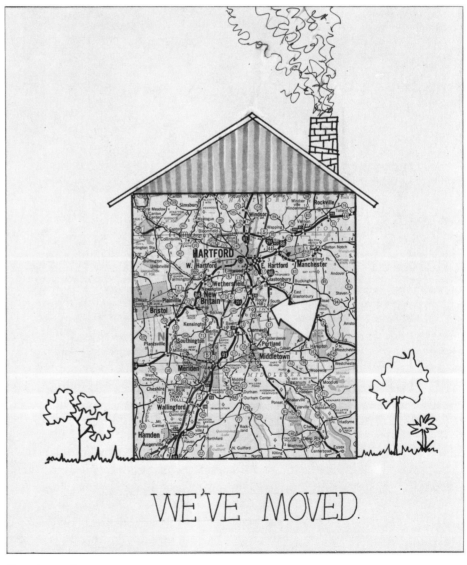

Blueprint moving announcement.

A spur of the moment sorority invitation made good use of the Xerox machine.

A very effective representation of the AZOCAL photo silk screen method.

Courtesy, George Zariff

For unto us
a Child is born,
unto us
a Son is given
And the government
shall be
upon His shoulder.
And His name
shall be called
Wonderful, Counsellor
The Mighty God,
the Everlasting Father,
The Prince of Peace.

Isaiah 9:6

AT PHIL'S
thurs. 8:00

CHAPTER 6
COLLAGE

No doubt everyone has kept a scrapbook at one time or another or collected memorabilia of some favorite subject, person or event. This in itself is a simple form of collage. You may find this to be an enjoyable, exciting method of card designing, particularly if drawing doesn't happen to be your forte. Besides, substituting scissors and glue for paint and ink provides a nice change of pace, less mess and preparation.

The greeting can be simply stated with a single, carefully-cropped photo, postcard print or magazine clipping pasted neatly on a single sheet of deckle-edged paper. Or you might really want to go all out and combine all sorts of materials, complemented with a sumptuous French folded card stock. Either way, always try to collect items appropriate for the occasion. Arrange bits of lace, embroidered ribbon, plush red velvet material, heart-shaped confections, possibly a few romantic photos or prints, for example, which could easily result in a unique Valentine's card. Carry through with a self-composed poem or take advantage of one in the reference books described in Chapter 4. Or instead of writing the message, why not incorporate it into the design by clipping and gluing the words from a magazine or pamphlet? Or, you may prefer to use transfer or press-type lettering. Your card may not secure a proposal, but guaranteed, the recipient will be duly impressed.

With the exception of the actual collage material, you should have most of the additional equipment already on hand from previous experiments. These will include rubber cement and thinner, Elmer's glue (or equivalent), scissors and various weights and shades of light colored and off-white paper, cut to size. Rubber cement may not be strong enough to hold with one application. However, a coating on each surface, allowed to dry before joining, will hold tenaciously. It is not recommended though, if permanency is a consideration. Even when coated on both card paper and clipping, the adhesive will begin to give way and turn yellow after a few months. But its facility of drying quickly, being easy to apply and remove, makes it ideal for fast, simple invitations and greeting cards. Elmer's glue, on the other hand, will adhere to just about anything, be it two or three-dimensional. Just be sure to give it sufficient time to dry.

A word of warning: as you begin to collect your collage material, it's going to become a real temptation to use everything. Employing too many items will make the design appear cluttered and jumbled. Select a nice variety of contrasting materials and save the rest for another design. Make several trial arrangements before actually gluing. When you've decided on the design you like best, arrange it on a spare piece of paper, then glue each item down on the cardpaper accordingly. As a final touch, don't hesitate to include some of your own artistic nuances; a fine delicate pen and ink Victorian frame would be an attractive complement for an old oval-cut photo, or, consider a more spontaneous eraser stamp or block print border.

Still another variation on the collage theme is to discard the scissors altogether and simply tear out your shapes. The rough edges will give your design a fresh, individual appearance. Most any paper can be used; newspaper, wrapping paper, metallic coated, fluorescent, tissue paper, construction paper, Color-aid paper, etc. Gather a wide assortment of surface textures, weights, patterns and colored scraps. Keep your shapes relatively simple for the sake of recognition. Incidentally, if you are using tissue or crepe paper, or any other of similar weight, you might try creasing or bunching the shapes during the gluing stage. Great way to add pattern and dimension to your card. I mention this also to buffer any discouragement should this happen accidentally, as it often does.

RUBBINGS

It has become quite the fad amongst vacationers and Sunday sight-seers to stop at historical cemeteries and take impressions of old gravestone epitaphs with large, waxy crayons and rice paper. If you are one of these people, then you've created what is known as a rubbing. For you non-gravestone impression-makers, a rubbing is made by placing a light-weight piece of paper over a raised, indented, or textured surface, then rubbing with pencil or crayon to pick up the image. So you can see by this definition that you don't have to feel limited to tombstones. In fact, your home and backyard alone hold a multitude of things that will create an endless variety of patterns. The trick is in recognizing them. Take a closer look at the floors, walls, the molding that frames the doors and windows, kitchen utensils (trivets make terrific rubbings), hardware tools, textured book bindings, buttons, lamp shades, wicker work or caned chair seats, cork, rug and curtain fringe, various cloths and braid, just to name a few. To these add some natural elements, such as leaves, twigs, flowers, grass, weeds, rocks, wood grain and bark, shells and feathers, to your collection. You might even include linoleum and woodcut blocks from previous printing endeavors or whatever else your eye picks up.

When you've assembled the objects that strike your fancy, think of an idea that will give them purpose. Using pencils of various shades of green to make impressions of clover leaves, for instance, would certainly produce an appropriate St. Patrick's Day party invitation. Top it off by gluing on a few real clover leaves or stencil a large stylized four leaf shape with sponge and paint. Abstract and freeform rubbings can easily be used to create imaginative Christmas ornaments, Easter eggs, or Mother's Day flowers.

After a short period of trial and error, you'll be able to automatically adjust the amount of pencil or crayon pressure needed to make the best image. Also experiment with various types of thin to medium weight paper stock: tissue paper, tracing paper, typewriter paper, vellum, rice paper, etc. Lithographic pencils, children's wax crayons or colored pencils usually produce the best results. When the rubbings have been completed, neatly trim and mount to a heavier card stock. Small dabs of glue in each corner will be sufficient. Include a message on the back or inside if desired.

Still another popular method of rubbing involves lighter fluid or benzine and an appropriate newspaper clipping. Squirt quite a bit of lighter fluid or benzine on the back of the clipping and let stand a few moments. To transfer the printed picture or copy, reverse the clipping and place face down on card stock. Then gently rub with a spoon or burnisher and remove. Make it a point to save the Sunday newspaper and supplements for a wider range of subjects to choose from, and the comics in color will really spice the imagination. Remember though, that the image will be reversed, so avoid type matter, and, one copy is all you can make with this method.

EMBOSSING

Embossing is a process of tooling on copper or aluminum foil which gives a design or picture the appearance of protruding from the surface of the card.

The professional tools and materials may be obtained from a hobby shop, but an old ball point pen or orange stick will do very nicely for most purposes. A thick newspaper or magazine makes an ideal working surface for the tooling operation.

First, choose a picture of the right size for your card, then cut out a piece of foil of that size. Place the foil, front side up, on your working surface. Put the picture over the foil and tape it down. With the pointed end of your working tool, trace the lines of the picture. Press hard enough to indent the foil but use care that you do not cut through it. Remove the picture from the foil and go over the design again to reinforce it, if necessary.

Now, turn over the foil and place it, front side down, on your working surface. The ridges made by the tracing will be visible. Trace the design again, but draw about 1/32 of an inch inside of your original lines. This tracing should be a little heavier than the first one. With the rounded end of your modeling tool, gently press the foil within the outlines of your design. Working thus from the reverse side of the foil is what creates the embossed surface of the design.

When the first embossing has been completed, turn the foil over, with the front side up, and place it on a hard surface. Retrace the original lines. Then, using the rounded end of your tool, flatten the background around the raised areas. Stroke lightly, and work toward the edges of the foil. Using each end of the tool as needed, continue to work on both the front and back of the foil until the design stands out from the background. When this is completed, cement the edges of the foil to your card.

If you wish to add color, use either enamel or oil paints. A thin coat of clear lacquer may be sprayed or painted over the finished picture for protection.

GRAPHIC BATIK

Surely everyone has used one of those variety store Easter Egg coloring kits. You know, the one that comes equipped with a clear wax crayon and a small assortment of food dyes. Remember how you could make simple, invisible, little patterns on each hard boiled egg before it was immersed into a bowl of hot food coloring. Half the fun was watching the design begin to take form as the egg began to color. Then they were neatly put aside on a plate or wire rack to dry until time and privacy were found to hide them.

But I have a simpler version based on the same principle that can be easily adapted to card designing, substituting a sturdy piece of paper for the egg, of course. And instead of food dyes, you can take advantage of watercolors and inks as well as a full, colorful, range of wax and oil crayons. Although I recommend watercolor paper to begin with, don't hesitate to experiment with other surface textures, possibly a slick coated stock or even acetate. Avoid soft, porous paper such as construction or rice paper, as it blots up the paint or ink too much.

When you've gathered the desired colors, take a large piece of white watercolor paper (15" x 20", at least) and attach the edges with masking tape to a piece of board or something equally inflexible. The next step is to section off the paper into card sizes. If your paper size is 15" x 20", for instance, you can divide the paper into twelve panels, each being 3" x 5"; or maybe four very long card shapes measuring 5" x 15"; or how 'bout eight 3" x 5" card sizes for the top two-thirds of the paper and two long, thin, horizontal panels on the bottom that will be 3" x 10" and so on. Once you've penciled in the size of the cards, lightly sketch in each design. You don't have to repeat the same idea. In fact, varying the image will make it more interesting for you. Let's say, four designs could be a snow-covered Tannenbaum, the following four could be a snowman family, the next four might be delicate snowflake patterns or a stained glass window design.

Once you've finally decided on and sketched out the pictures, then you're ready to draw in the shapes and lines with crayon. For the strongest image, it's best to use light colored crayons (white, yellows, pinks, oranges, etc.) with dark water colors, or vice versa. Incidentally, using just a white crayon and dark blue and purple inks is great for creating quick snow scenes.

When you've completed crayoning, take a large watercolor brush and completely saturate the paper with clear water. Now apply the selected inks and water colors; the crayon will resist the liquid coloring just as it did on the Easter egg. Blend purple-blues for a rich sky effect or bright pinks, reds and yellows for a more festive mood, and maybe even dab a contrasting color to accent a shape here and there. If you've made a stained glass window design; you could have a ball with all kinds of color. And don't feel limited to just a brush, stippling the paint or ink with a toothbrush as you did in the stencil chapter will introduce a nice contrast in texture or try blotting the paper here and there with a sponge to control values, or use whatever else strikes your fancy.

When the painting has been completed, allow the paper to dry thoroughly, the masking tape will keep it from buckling. When dry, remove masking tape, cut and mount each design on a medium-weight paper stock of complementary color. By all means include a message, or other ornamentation.

Rubber cement batik method was
used for this Christmas design.

Naturally, there are many variations to this technique. I hope you get a chance to try them all. You have already been introduced to one method described in Chapter 5 "Block Printing Without Blocks," in which white poster paint can be used to replace the crayon. The only exception in the procedure is to let the paint dry completely before applying waterproof ink. After the ink has thoroughly dried, you place the mounted watercolor paper under the bathtub faucet and gently run luke-warm water over the white poster paint areas until all the paint has been removed. The lines and shapes will be a lot crisper, sharper, a nice contrast in character from the crayon.

Still another Batik technique is done with rubber cement replacing paint and crayon. This method tends to have the element of surprise on its side as it is more difficult to control. However, this is what makes the procedure exciting and the artwork more individual. Once again, follow the same steps in preparing the paper and making the light pencil sketches. Then take the brush from the jar or can of rubber cement and dribble as nearly as possible to the shapes of your sketch. How quickly you move the brush will determine the weight of the line, a very slow motion will naturally allow more cement to drop, thus making a wider line. Varying the consistency of the cement with thinner will also have an effect on weight and control. After a few trial experiments, however, you'll be able to gauge speed, amount and consistency to suit your fancy. In addition to dribbling, try brushing on a cement texture. I have a friend who uses this brush-cement method exclusively for creating furry things: animals, coats or feathers, and it works. Since one inspiration usually leads to another, I'm sure it won't be long before you've accumulated a fine batch of tools and techniques you can pass on.

Needless to say, once the rubber cement has dried (it will appear dull and somewhat opaque), simply proceed as you have done before. When the ink or paint has dried, the rubber cement can be easily rubbed off, leaving a clean pattern of shapes on the colored paper.

Smudging your oil crayons will produce a soft smooth effect — similar in touch and appearance to flower petals.

LETTERPRESS

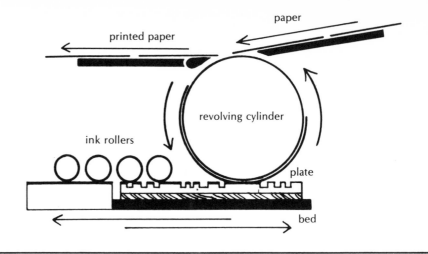

Cross section of letterpress plate

OFFSET LITHOGRAPHY

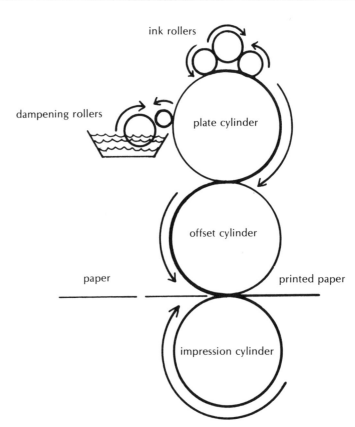

Cross section of offset lithographic plate

GRAVURE

Cross section of gravure plate

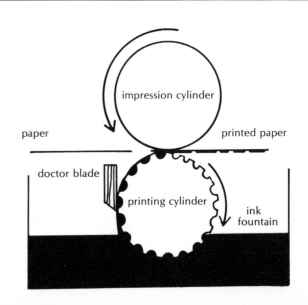

110

CHAPTER 7
PREPARING ART FOR COMMERCIAL PRINTING

Maybe much of what I've said so far hasn't really been up your alley. It's fun to receive hand-made cards, but you'd rather concentrate on the artistic problems of creating the original art work and prefer to leave the reproduction of it up to the printer. Then you're with the large majority of artists who design their own cards.

However, that doesn't mean that printers can successfully cope with just anything you bring them. (A local printer I know flatly refuses to accept any amateur Christmas card printing jobs, "too many headaches.") You can save the printer, and yourself, a lot of grief or disappointment, with a basic understanding of the printing processes.

In this chapter I'll run down the basics of the various printing methods, how mechanicals are prepared for one, two, three or four color printing, scaling pictures so you can fit a four foot canvas on a four inch card, selecting and fitting type, and show you examples of some of the results.

First, the presses.

Letterpress

This is the oldest method, and many local printers still use this equipment. Printing is accomplished by means of a metal plate into which the design has been etched. In letterpress the image to be printed is "raised", (or rather, the area not to be printed is recessed) then inked on the raised surface, and brought into direct contact with the paper. It's much the same effect as using a rubber stamp.

Offset Lithography

This method employs a different approach to printing. The plate never comes into direct contact with the paper, but the curved plate is brought into contact with an intermediate rubber-covered cylinder which receives the inked image and transfers (or "offsets") it by contact to a third cylinder over which the paper passes.

Gravure

You're not as apt to have access to this kind of printing, but you should know its principle, which is most nearly like printing an etching. This makes it just the opposite of letterpress. Instead of inking the raised surfaces, the ink is forced into the recessed areas and the plate surface wiped clean. The plate is then printed under enough pressure to lift the ink out of the recesses onto the paper. The deeper the recess the more ink it holds and the deeper the black (or color) will be in that area.

HOW TO MAKE A MECHANICAL

If the word "mechanical" is turning you off already, bear with me for just this page. We're not going to get technical. All you need to know is how to give the artwork to the printer in a form he can work from.

Black and white artwork will be reproduced in one of two ways.

1.   If the artwork is all done with just blacks or whites, it can be reproduced in "line."

Line art has only black or white areas. Cross hatching, stipples, drybrush or other shading effects are made up of black lines.

2.   If your design includes some areas of intermediate greys, it must be reproduced as a "halftone." That requires photographing the original through a screen which breaks up the photo image into dots. The dots are larger and closer together in dark areas; they're smaller and farther apart in light areas. These dots, hardly visible to the eye, are etched into the printing plate, which when inked, reproduces the *effect* of a tone, even though made up of a multitude of small black and white dots.

Any original artwork containing intermediate grey tones must be photographed through a halftone screen. Here is a portion of a screened halftone and an enlarged section.

Let's take the simplest kind of design and prepare it to be printed. Since you won't want things crooked, you'll need to work on a drawing board with a T-square and a triangle. Draw the size and shape of the borders on the paper and then the placement and size of the design.

Do this with a blue pencil so it won't be picked up when photographed. We'll start with drawing for a Christmas card, 12 inches high. It is to be printed as a halftone at 5" high. The drawing should be photostated to that size and rubber cemented into position so the printer will know both the desired size and placement of the artwork. (You'll find the nearest photostat service in the yellow pages and their services are not expensive).

Don't worry about the quality of the photostat. It is only used as a guide. The printer will also need your original artwork to make his halftone copy.

Here the lettering was done by hand at exact size, right in position. This will be photographed in line. (If you had the lettering set in type, a proof of it would be rubber cemented into position. We'll talk more about type later in this chapter.

Original art, marked for reduction.

To 5"

Designed by Walt Reed

Greeting Card, as printed.

Mechanical with instructions as written for the printer. Either a photostat reduced to size or traced outline in red will position the art for the platemaker.

Merry Christmas

from the

Reeds

Lettering can be done by hand or in type and may be printed in another color if so designated.

Dropout Halftone print black

Merry Christmas

from the

Reeds

Lettering 100% Process Red

4"

5½"

Key drawing in black and white.
Register marks, placed on the margins.

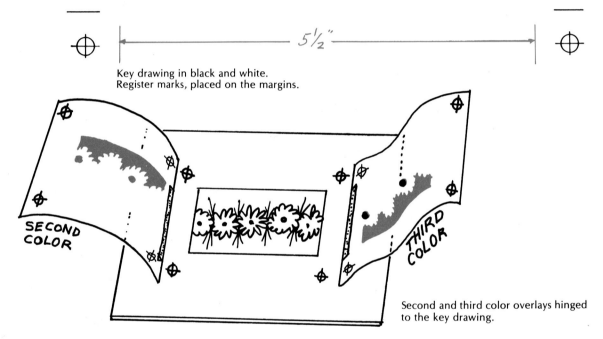

SECOND COLOR

THIRD COLOR

Second and third color overlays hinged
to the key drawing.

The finished printing, made from the
separate drawings, printed in sequence.

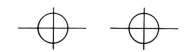

Adding Color by Overlays

If you're working on a budget (and who isn't?) you can save a lot of the printer's time, and your cost, by doing some of his work for him. That is, you can pre-separate the colors in your artwork. Let's assume you have a design you want to print in black, blue and yellow. Each color will require a separate drawing.

First, the key drawing is made in black. Usually this drawing will carry the main portion of the design and will be printed in black in final reproduction. Next come the important register marks. Usually four of them are drawn on the margins just outside the area that will be trimmed off.

Drawings for the areas to be printed in each of the two colors must have the same kind of register marks, in exactly the same position in relation to the art. This will allow printing the plates for the additional colors in proper position with the key drawing and with each other.

If you should have a light box, or can improvise one with a strong light under a sheet of frosted glass, you can readily align your drawings. Make your first key drawing on translucent bond paper so the light will shine through it. Attach a second piece of bond paper over the first, draw register marks exactly over those on the key drawing. Next draw the design areas to be printed in blue — using black ink. Repeat the same process for yellow areas, again using black ink. The printer will make a line plate of each drawing, but use blue and yellow inks on the designated plates in printing.

Why use black? Because it reproduces accurately and no special filters will be required when the platemaker photographs it. Using black instead of the actual color may seem like working in the dark, but if you've begun with a color sketch as a guide, you should have a good mental picture of what you want.

An alternative method, especially if your original black and white drawing is on opaque illustration board, is to use transparent acetate overlays, as illustrated.

Position a sheet of acetate over your key drawing and tape it securely along the top or one side. Plan your other overlay to hings from another side. Use a "treated" acetate so the ink will adhere properly and add the register marks over those on the key art. Now, as before, draw the design areas you want to appear in the second color, in black. (Or you can use red, which photographs as black). Finally, make the third overlay for the third color. The final printed result may look even better than you expected!

YELLOW

YELLOW AND RED

The proofs across the top of the page are known as "progressives." That is, beginning with yellow, each color is surprinted in the above order as a test of the proper relationships of the colors to each other. The four-color proof on the right, represents the final printed result.

RED

BLUE

The row of illustrations on the left are the individual color separations as produced by the screened films. Each is proofed like this by the platemaker to check the quality of the engraving.

BLACK

Courtesy, Looart Press, Inc.
Designed by Joseph Russo

YELLOW, RED AND BLUE   YELLOW, RED, BLUE AND BLACK

Full Color Separations

Let's assume for a moment that money is no object. You've got a great painting for a greeting card design and want to have it reproduced in full color. What kind of process does it go through to get printed? We'll take a professional example as a kind of case history.

Virtually all full color printing is done with just four inks, a magenta red, a cyan blue, a strong lemon yellow, and black.

To reproduce the colors of the painting, it is first photographed through a series of filters, on black and white film — an orange filter to retain only the blues on film, a green filter for reds and a violet for the yellows. The black is slightly filtered with yellow/orange. These produce unscreened negatives.

Next, a screen is interposed, its pattern varied according to color, and each angled differently so the halftone dots can cover each other in varying degrees to produce all the color nuances.

Under magnification, you can see the individual dots of pure color, but to the normal eye it all merges together to create the effect of color mixtures (Like pointillism). The black plate is added to give the reproduction a little more "snap" by reinforcing the dark areas and details of modelling.

If you've commissioned the printing yourself, you will be shown the progressive proofs for your approval before the actual printing is done. It is still possible for the engraver to make minor color adjustments in the film or plates at this stage, prior to the actual printing.

As I've indicated above, this is an expensive process, beyond the means of most of us for a personal card. But, since all four color printing goes through this procedure it is good to be knowledgeable about it, especially if you are ambitious to pursue a professional career as a greeting card artist.

Courtesy, Looart Press, Inc.

The watercolor technique lends
itself beautifully to designs
using subtle color changes and
muted contrasts.

Designed by Linda Powell   Courtesy, Looart Press, Inc.

This design relies on strong contrasts to differentiate between interior and exterior. Either acrylics or designer's colors could be used for this approach.

Professional Examples

I'd like to inspire you on the next few pages with some examples of excellent contemporary greeting card designs. They are all the product of a young, progressive firm, Looart Press, with the imprint of Current, Inc., in Boulder, Colorado.

Some of the designs could only be reproduced by four-color separations as I've just described to you. However, in others, the artists have used the same materials and design methods presented earlier in the book. The only difference is that they've been reproduced in thousands of copies, on printing presses, while yours will probably be printed by hand methods for a relatively small number of copies.

Designed by Linda Powell   Courtesy, Looart Press, Inc.

The spatter background provides an effective textural foil for the pine needles and the old-fashioned toys in the foreground.

Torn paper collage, reinforced with outlined shapes creates an informal, good-humored design for one of a series of "fun bug notes."

Designed by Marsha Howe
Courtesy, Looart Press, Inc.

Above, acrylic colors are bright and dry quickly. Here, the lamb and lion are posed to convey the inside message of, "Peace."

To the right, is one of a series of "leaflet" covers. When you plan designs, look for unusual or unique ingredients that will add interest to your design. Here the dragon fly provides that extra touch.

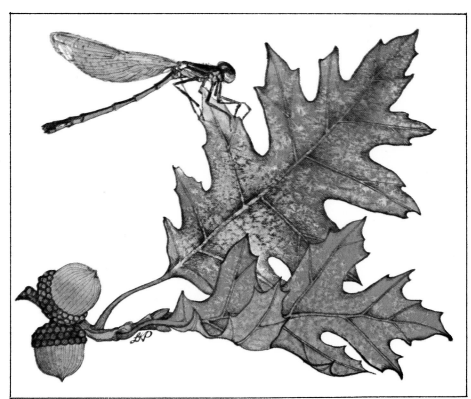

Designed by Linda Powell   Courtesy, Looart Press, Inc.

Designed by Joseph Russo

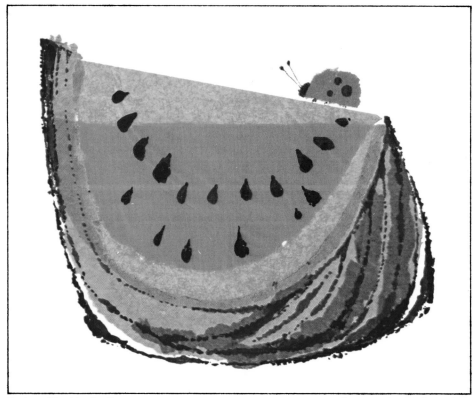

Designed by Marsha Howe

Humor in greeting cards can range from gentle whimsy to savage satire. Studio cards are in a special category and oftentimes go to extremes that most traditional publishers avoid. Some areas of studio and traditional humor overlap however, and more and more publishers have both lines.

Designed by Joseph Russo   Courtesy, Looart Press, Inc.

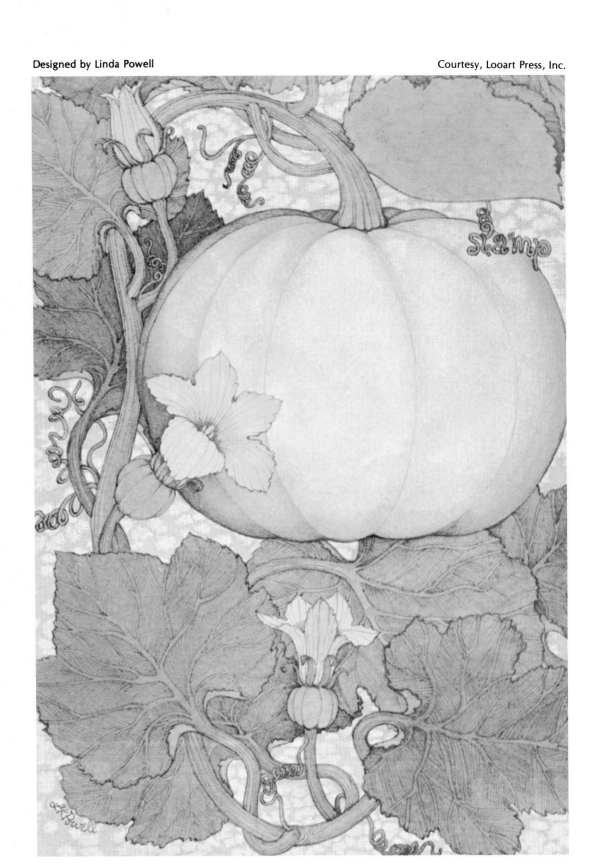

Greeting card publishers print a wide variety of related items such as the colorful self-mailing note card, above, envelopes, recipe cards, calendars and post cards. Good art and fresh ideas are always welcomed.

Designed by Heidi Brandt   Courtesy, Looart Press, Inc.

The Kingdom of GOD is JUSTICE PEACE Joy
ROMANS 14-17

Colored tissue paper, construction paper and patterned textiles are all effective collage materials as successfully combined here.

A potato cross section, art gum eraser or a rounded piece of styrofoam can be easily incised and printed to spell out an appropriate message.

Designed by George Zariff

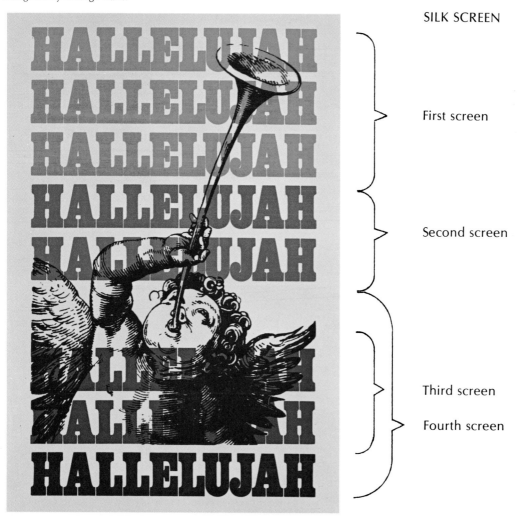

SILK SCREEN

First screen

Second screen

Third screen

Fourth screen

The sequence of printing the above design has been carefully planned for superimposing the cherub and bottom line of type as the fourth screen.

Courtesy, Conception Abbey Press

Again, the sequence of color permits printing a darker color and value over a lighter one, preserving the brilliance of color.

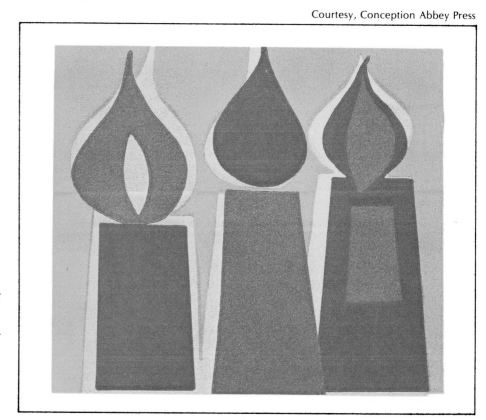

Crayon Resist

This is a form of graphic batik as described on page 107. It requires some planning first, but can be easily repeated. After the crayoned areas have been filled in, cover the whole shape with India ink. Once the ink has dried, simply scrape off the ink where desired, revealing the crayon beneath. You can work back and forth to make changes, but part of the charm is in taking advantage of accidental effects.

Found Objects

Once you get started with using found objects for printing, there'll be no stopping you. I bought the stalk of broccoli to cook, but after a fresh look at it, something clicked and I took it from the kitchen to the studio for a trial print. With the bagged base and message, it made a perfect Arbor Day motif.

Monoprint

Because a monoprint (as its name implies) makes but one print, the design must be repainted each time. A time-saver here, was to make an art gum eraser stamp for the stars and simply print them in position when the blue area had dried.

With an international theme like postage stamps, you might want to use some of the various ways in which "Merry Christmas" is expressed around the world. Here are eighteen different examples.

God Jul (Swedish). **Feliz Natal** (Brazilian). **Glaedelig Jul** (Danish). **Joyeaux Noel** (French). **Bona Natale** (Italian). **Boas Festas** (Portuguese). **Hauskaa Joulua** (Finnish). **Hartelyke Kerstgroeten** (Dutch). **Kung Hsi Hsin** (Chinese). **Felices Pascuas** (Spanish). **Nosteria Lui Christ's Sa Va Die De Felos** (Rumanian). **Prijemne Svatky** or **Vesele Vanoce** (Czech). **Froehliche Weinachten** (German). **Kala Christougenia** (Greek). **Christmas O-medeto** (Japanese). **Glaedelig Jul** (Norwegian). **Wesolych Swiat** (Polish). **S. Rozhdestvom Chirstova** (Russian). **Sretan Bozoic** (Serbian). **Merry Christmas** (English).

A simple cutout shape for the cover reveals a colorful pattern of stamps arranged in a Christmas tree shape beneath.

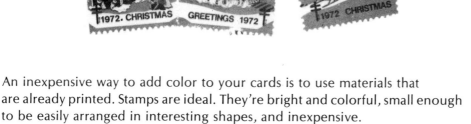

An inexpensive way to add color to your cards is to use materials that are already printed. Stamps are ideal. They're bright and colorful, small enough to be easily arranged in interesting shapes, and inexpensive.

If you have a collector in the family, you should be able to obtain lots of the duplicates of little or no value, but perfect for your use. Otherwise, your local stamp dealer can supply mixed packets of colorful stamps at very low prices.

This will also give you an added use for the annual Christmas or Easter seals from charitable organizations, such as the National Tuberculosis and Respiratory Disease Association.

With tracing paper laid over the art work, draw a diagonal line from the lower left through the upper right hand corner. Measure off the dimension desired along the base and draw a vertical line to intersect with the diagonal line. Another line, parallel with the base, intersecting at the same point, will complete the new rectangle in perfect proportion with the first. This procedure is the same whether you want to reduce or enlarge the original picture.

An irregularly shaped subject can also be enlarged or reduced in scale by first ruling off the rectangle bordering the outer edges of the shapes and then drawing the diagonal through the corners.

A light box will enable you to refine drawings through successive tracings, also helps in aligning overlays and type in making mechanicals.

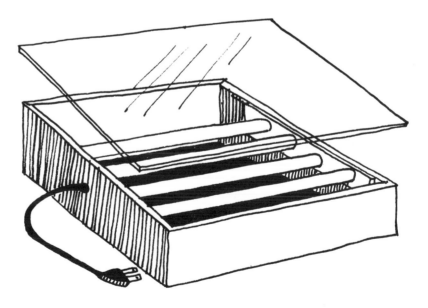

Scaling

Let's assume you've done a painting that would make an ideal subject for a printed Christmas card. Its dimensions are 16" x 20". You'd like to know how to reduce it in proportion to be printed on a 5" x 6" card.

Start by placing a sheet of tracing paper over your painting and draw a rectangle the same size. Then, draw a diagonal line through the lower left and upper right corners of the rectangle.

You can reduce the picture at any place along this diagonal and it will be in proportion with the original. By drawing a horizontal and vertical line which meet at a point on the diagonal 5 inches from the left margin, you will find that the picture will scale to 4" x 5". If you place the traced 4" x 5" rectangle over the 5" x 6" card size, you'll see that you can frame the reduced painting with a half inch margin all around.

Should you want to enlarge a small subject, use the same procedure with a diagonal line. In this case, the diagonal should extend beyond the rectangle of the original artwork.

If your design is an irregular shape, you can enlarge or reduce it by the same method by just ruling a rectangle around the four outer edges.

Indicate the dimensions wanted on the tracing. The printer can take it from there. Simple enough?

The light box

A light box is a marvelous aid for any artist and can save a lot of time by enabling you to make changes or refinements in your drawings through successive tracings. (It is necessary to work on drawing or tracing paper thin enough for the light to shine through).

If your local art supply store doesn't carry one, or if you would simply like to save the expense, a light box can be easily improvised. It is no more than a light behind a glass. Frosted glass is best because it diffuses the light evenly and fluorescent lights are preferable, since they spread out the light over an area larger than a light bulb.

Make the corners of the light box square so it can be used with a T-square and a triangle. This will enable you to keep your layouts or mechanicals accurate.

ABCDEFGHIJKLMNOPQRSTUVWXYZ

abcdefghijklmnopqrstuvwxyz **1234567890$&()/**

HELVETICA   SEMI-BOLD   16 POINT

AAAAAAAAAAAAAAAA

192 point (phototype)   72 point   6 point

TYPES AND SIZES

Type generally comes in a range of sizes (or heights) from 6 to 72 points. (There are 72 points to an inch.) If other sizes are needed, with phototype or photostats, type can be made virtually any height for special requirements. Type in a line is measured by picas, with approximately 6 picas to an inch.

You can order type through your local printer or from a typographer. They will have a specimen book of their various type faces and sizes to choose from.

A letterpress printer may set the type from his own stock. A typographer will furnish a set of proofs of the type for reproduction. These "repro" proofs are to be mounted into proper position on the mechanical for reproduction in line.

So, after you've picked a type style at the size you want, the trick is to know how much room it will take, or better, to know how to order the right size to fit into a predetermined space.

Let's say you have a large family and want a Christmas greeting that will name everyone in it, including the dog and cat. You have a space under the illustration of approximately 3 inches by 2 inches. Start by printing or typing out the copy and counting the characters. Here is a hypothetical family message:

> Best wishes for Christmas and the New Year from the Evarts :
> Susan, Joe, Joe, Jr., Irene, and Alice.
> Rover and Mehitibel join in.

The character count, including punctuation marks and spaces between words is 128.

Pica Rule

Alphabets come in all kinds of shapes and sizes. Not all printers or typographers have every type face, but they should be able to provide a range of styles from which to choose one appropriate to your design.

You might have selected Times Roman, a good, classic typeface. To start with, 12 point type looks about right. In this size, 13 lower case characters will fit in one inch. With three inches of space, we can fit 39 characters into one line. If the type were set solid, it would look like this:

> Best wishes for Christmas and the New
> Year from the Evarts : Susan, Joe, Joe, Jr.
> Irene, Alice. Rover and Mehitibel join in.

Obviously, we have more depth available which will allow setting each of the family member's names on an individual line. By giving a layout to the printer, with clear instructions about the type face, size and length of lines, he can provide the type or a repro proof in this form:

> Best wishes for Christmas and the New
> Year from the Evarts
> Susan
> Joe
> Joe, Jr.
> Irene
> Alice
> Rover and
> Mehitibel
> join in.

We now fit the type into the designated space. If you need to get more fully into the subject of type, mechanicals and copy casting, there are several good books available. See the bibliography for a listing.

Designed by Marsha Howe   Courtesy, Looart Press, Inc.

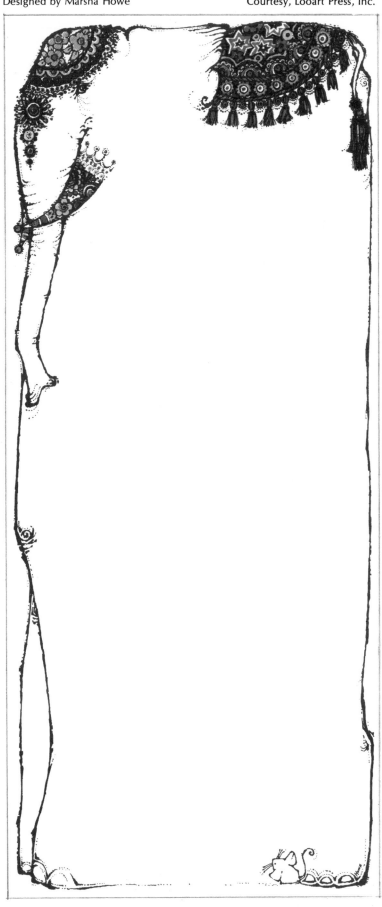

Letter writing buffs will appreciate the simple, but decorative elephant design. The elongated shape complies beautifully with the shape of the extra long stationery sheets.

CHAPTER 8
GOING PROFESSIONAL

I'm sure many of you who have sent homemade cards to friends and relatives have sometimes gotten a response similar to, "Boy, that's great! have you ever thought of doing this professionally?" No doubt the thought had crossed your mind at one time or another. The extra money is certainly incentive enough, but it also gives one a nice feeling of professionalism. The problem of turning your skill to profit should be approached with ordinary common sense. Let's face it, you won't be "discovered" and make a fortune overnight, nor will you have an "easy" job at home. The degree of effort, talent, study and research you put into the creation of your artwork will determine your success in selling it to a greeting card company. And believe me, the trained eye of the publisher can spot a "quickie" creation dashed off in odd moments a mile away.

The best way to know what type of greeting card art is in demand is to simply study the merchandise being sold. Be aware of trends. Ask your friends and relatives what they like to see in a greeting card design. Retailers, too, can be very helpful by describing preferences indicated by customers.

Carefully examine design and sentiment in relation to the occasion. Observe the color, medium, technique, even the shape of the card being used to convey various moods and events.

A vertical shaped card seems to be the most preferred, no doubt one of the reasons being that it takes less space to display than a horizontal one. On the subject of medium and technique, you should give some attention to the traditional greeting card. These conventional, usually realistic renderings of mother and child, snow and seascapes, floral studies and wide-eyed, bushy-tailed baby cats, dogs and rabbits, still corner a good portion of the market with studio cards running a close second in volume and popularity. Watercolor has always been a favorite medium, although designer's colors, opaques, pastels, colored inks and dyes are acceptable, by themselves or combined. Oil paintings don't seem to be as desirable, partly because of their size and bulk; however, acrylics which can resemble oils in appearance are well received because of their versatility.

Designed by Linda Powell

Courtesy, Looart Press, Inc.

Thinking of you

A traditional approach, but lifted far above the average treatment by a careful artistic rendering from nature.

It requires a good deal more skill and training to create a realistic representation of objects, people or scenes than the highly stylized shapes and compositions we've been involved with. Most professional greeting card artists have had some formal art school training. Still with persistence and practice, nothing's impossible. In the long run, you may feel more comfortable holding a watercolor brush than a printing brayer and better at it too.

The necessary equipment is far less varied and complex, but the results of your efforts will only match the quality of your tools. Good quality watercolor brushes and paper for instance, are required for decent results. Cheap materials will only use up unnecessary time, paper, paint and patience. Naturally, the surface texture of the board or paper should befit the technique. A rough surface would be suitable for brush and ink or watercolor, but not for pen and ink. The smoother surfaces permit finer detail.

The how-to aspects depend on where your interests lie. There are a large number of instructive books on the market or possibly in your local library that cover just about every theory and technique, be it classical or contemporary, on all the popular subjects and mediums. If you feel competent with, say, watercolors rather than opaques, then you should naturally submit work in the medium to which you feel best suited. This applies to subject matter as well. You may find you have a special ability to do flowers instead of figures or landscapes instead of animals, etc. But do your utmost not to

Designed by Linda Powell
Courtesy, Looart Press, Inc.

A wet-in-wet watercolor technique creates the soft, furry effect of this playful ball of fluff.

Should you have a warm spot in your heart for nostalgia, scrounge around the attic or knick-knack shops for antique items that tell their story.

Designed by Linda Powell

Courtesy, Looart Press, Inc.

Designed by Edvard Johnson

Courtesy, Douglas Van Dorn, Ltd.

The fine arts lend themselves beautifully to greeting cards and many museums and galleries reproduce their paintings for the purpose. Here is an excellent church exterior interpreted in acrylics.

limit yourself; the more diversification, the more likelihood of a sale or an assignment. Use what you see on the market as a basis, a guide for your card designs, not an absolute. Besides the traditional mediums and techniques, hope you will include samples made by some of the printing methods described in the previous chapters; utilize your own style and flair. Avoid submitting artwork unrelated to card designs, such as an oil painting of the family or art school sketches, etc.

Designed by Claude Croney   Courtesy, Douglas Van Dorn, Ltd.

Many artists who are not otherwise involved with greeting card art, sell the reproduction rights to certain of their paintings. Here, a landscape subject provides an original artistic departure from the more traditional Christmas or New Year's themes.

This, however, doesn't mean you shouldn't be aware of, and even get involved with, "allied products". This is merchandise related to greeting card design such as calendars, books, bookmarks, decorations for Christmas, Halloween, birthdays, wrapping paper, posters, tags, tallies, postcards, stationery, note cards and envelopes. Letter and note paper design, for instance, is a real up-and-coming sideline of greeting card design. In addition to an array of attractive colors to write on, fresh, imaginative things are being done with letter and notepaper graphics. Mod decorative borders, whimsical animals and bugs, delicate flowers, among other things, are being used to make letter writing more personal and exciting. In fact, the variety of style and subject matter has become so extensive it's nearly impossible not to find something to fit your character and interests. Topics covering nature, special holiday and personal events, contemporary issues including ecology, politics, home interests and hobbies, etc., leave the door open for all kinds of techniques.

Of course, only original material should be submitted, copying or adapting another artist's work could result in real legal hassle. This is also a good time

Designed by Linda Powell
Courtesy, Looart Press, Inc.

The pencil is a more versatile drawing medium than most people realize. It can be used to create anything from hard-edged, rough objects like rocks, to soft, gentle things like this sleeping fawn.

Designed by Linda Powell   Courtesy, Looart Press, Inc.

Pen and ink can be just as flexible and enjoyable. Experiment with different pen points and paper surface.

Designed by Andrea DaRif

This handsome pen and ink rendering was reproduced on a gold metallic paper stock for a very elegant touch.

to talk about protecting your own rights. One of the most prevalent fears of beginners is that their submitted ideas or designs may be stolen by an unscrupulous publisher. This is an extremely unlikely possibility.

Most publishers are ethical and would be only too pleased to find, and pay for, a saleable idea or design and, let's face it, most beginners' designs are not professional enough to tempt stealing, even if a publisher were dishonest! However, there is a very simple way to protect yourself. The magic word is copyright. This form of protection is provided by the law of the United States (Title 17, U.S. Code) to authors of literary, dramatic, musical, artistic, and other intellectual works. The Library of Congress Copyright Office Circular states that the owner of a copyright is granted by law certain exclusive rights in his work such as:

> The right to print, reprint and copy the work.
> The right to sell or distribute copies of the work.

This right covers your roughs as well as the finished product. You, as the author or artist, are the only one who can claim copyright: unless, of course, you give up your right voluntarily to the recipient of your work.

To invoke this protection, have a rubber stamp made including the year and your name, as follows: © 1974, Susan Evarts. Stamp this on a corner of any idea sketches or finished designs you submit. This will prevent their being published without your permission. Naturally, if you make a sale, his purchase order would require your granting greeting card reproduction rights to the publisher.

Courtesy, Looart Press, Inc.

You may prefer to specialize in a single area, such as wildlife or flora and fauna. The varieties of birds, fish, and fur subjects to choose from defies count.

That just about covers *what* to submit; now let's consider *how* to present your card designs. It rates just as much attention. Requirements vary from company to company. Many art directors, for instance, would prefer finished art; by that I mean, as perfect in detail as those reproduced on the market. Others favor sketches or roughs. Color transparencies are required by still other publishers. Then you have art directors who want the artist to write them before sending samples, to learn about size, printing requirements and general guidelines. Some art directors find "dummy art" the most suitable way to assess greeting card designs. These are full color designs mounted or actually done on standard size card folders to simulate the finished product.

There are also differences in technical requirements. Generally, designs are printed by offset lithography in four to six colors. When preparing finished art, give thoughtful consideration to bleed, slightly extending the borders of your artwork to accomodate the printer for cropping or trimming the edges. Normally, this should be a minimum of ⅛". An acetate overlay will be required should you want to include any extra ornamentation: gold, silver, glitter or sparkle, etc. This also applies to any solid color, be it an outline or area.

For the ecology minded, rendering a subject on behalf of an endangered species, such as the coyote, printed on 100% recycled paper provides a way to do your bit.

Designed by Linda Powell
Courtesy, Looart Press, Inc.

As a rule, finished lettering need not be done by the freelance artist unless it is an integral part of the design. Most companies have staff members who will handle captions and sentiment. However, you should allow sufficient space within each cover design for easy placement of the greeting. Use a tracing paper overlay to indicate size, style and placement. Finally, keep your designs and color treatments *simple*. Putting too much into any one creation usually results in a confusing, cluttered design. Common sense tells you that smaller cards (4½" x 6⅜" or 4⅛" x 6 11/16") selling for 25¢ should be much simpler in design and embellishment than larger cards (5⅜" x 7⅝" or 4 9/16" x 8½") going for 50¢ and up.

Now let's get down to the nitty-gritty of price since that's basically what it's all about. Dollars and cents, like previously mentioned requirements, will vary with each company. The amount usually depends on the merit of the idea, quality and amount of work involved. A beginning freelancer can expect around $30 to $40 or more for finished art work including cover design and some appropriate inside treatment. Naturally, very involved special designs or exceptional ideas will command higher rates. Needless to say, as a beginner, your toils won't be rewarded very much. But take heart, rates usually increase with your experience.

To learn about their layout and technical requirements, I'd recommend that you write to individual greeting card companies for specifics. The best way to do this is to consult the library business indexes for names and addresses. In addition to contacting individual companies, you might get in touch with the National Association of Greeting Card Publishers (NAGCP) and Gift Wrappings and Tyings Association (GWTA). They publish a small booklet listing names, addresses, general suggestions and requirements of most greeting card companies. This pamphlet, "The Artists and Writers Market List," is available by writing to NAGCP or GWTA, 200 Park Avenue, Pan Am Building, New York, N.Y. 10017. As a novice freelancer, you should also take advantage of the booklet "Dialogues" for some worthwhile information on greeting card verse writing (also from the NAGCP address). Always address your correspondence to the "Art Director" if no

In addition to traditional or nostalgic objects, keep an eye open for old magazines and illustrated books. There is a wealth of old illustrations that can be reproduced to celebrate almost any occasion. These antique ornaments, for example, were taken from "The Crystal Palace Illustrated Catalogue" of 1851.

If your interests lie in woodcuts, you're sure to appreciate these old woodcut initials from an early sixteenth century alphabet.

One of my favorite renditions of Kris Kringle is Thomas Nast's "Merry Old Santa Claus" from Harper's Weekly, 1881.

definite name is given. This allows the mail room to direct it to the proper person in the shortest time. Leave plenty of time for a reply — sometimes as much as six weeks. Letters should be kept short, to the point and business-like, no matter if sent alone or accompanying art samples. In the event you happen to live near a greeting card company, by all means personally contact the publisher. Be sure to telephone the art director for an appointment.

In conclusion, your greeting card samples should always be neatly flapped with plain brown paper, tissue, or visualizing paper, legibly identified with your full name and address. And finally, to facilitate prompt consideration and return of your material, be sure to include sufficient return postage.

You're on your own now . . . Happy sales!

Simple abstract and freeform shapes have been repeated to produce this unusual wrapping paper design. Pages 60-61 in the Block Printing chapter demonstrate how this can be done.

Designed by Marsha Howe
Courtesy, Looart Press, Inc.

French Strawberry Pie

(Serves 6 to 8)

1 baked 9" pie shell
1 3-oz. pkg. cream cheese
3 tablespoons cream
1 quart strawberries
1 cup sugar
1 cup whipping cream
2 tablespoons cornstarch
few drops lemon juice

Blend the cream cheese and cream until soft and smooth. Spread over the cooled pie shell. Wash and hull the berries. Select one half of the best ones. If they are large, slice in half. Add the sugar to the rest and let stand until juicy. Mash and rub through a sieve. Mix this puree with the cornstarch. Add a few drops of lemon juice. Cook this mixture until thick and transparent, stirring constantly. Cool and put half over the cream cheese. Arrange the berries in the sauce, then pour the remaining puree over the berries and chill. To serve, top with sweetened whipped cream.

A clever and novel combination of a recipe note card and post card. This is a way to share a favorite recipe with a special greeting.

Being a constant jotter-downer, I find these memos or note pads a real necessity. Notice how well the phone design utilizes the space.

Designed by Marsha Howe
Courtesy, Looart Press, Inc.

Here are examples of some of the many related items produced by greeting card publishers, all of which employ the talents of artists and designers.

Designed by Linda Powell

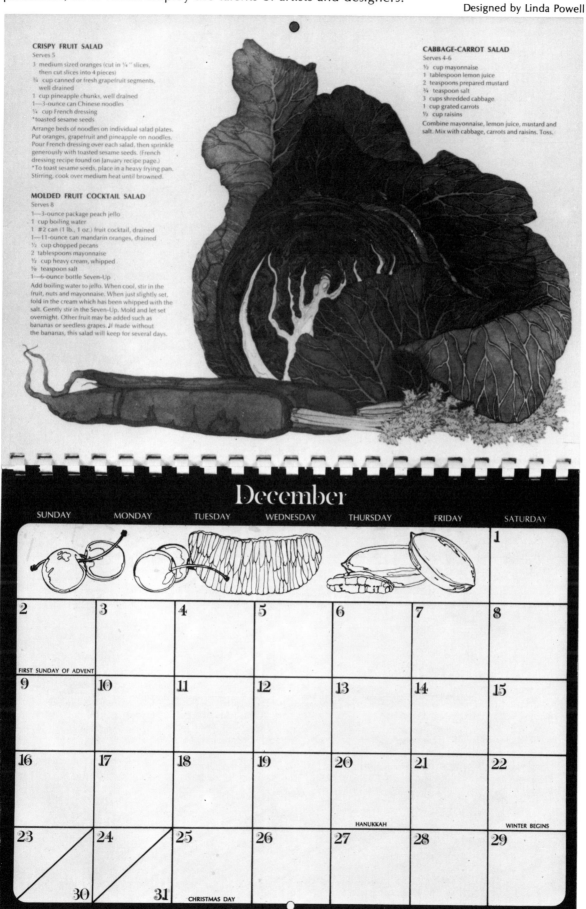

CRISPY FRUIT SALAD
Serves 5

3 medium sized oranges (cut in ¼" slices,
  then cut slices into 4 pieces)
¾ cup canned or fresh grapefruit segments,
  well drained
1 cup pineapple chunks, well drained
1—3-ounce can Chinese noodles
¼ cup French dressing
*toasted sesame seeds

Arrange beds of noodles on individual salad plates.
Put oranges, grapefruit and pineapple on noodles.
Pour French dressing over each salad, then sprinkle
generously with toasted sesame seeds. (French
dressing recipe found on January recipe page.)
*To toast sesame seeds, place in a heavy frying pan.
Stirring, cook over medium heat until browned.

MOLDED FRUIT COCKTAIL SALAD
Serves 8

1—3-ounce package peach jello
1 cup boiling water
1 #2 can (1 lb., 1 oz.) fruit cocktail, drained
1—11-ounce can mandarin oranges, drained
½ cup chopped pecans
2 tablespoons mayonnaise
½ cup heavy cream, whipped
⅛ teaspoon salt
1—6-ounce bottle Seven-Up

Add boiling water to jello. When cool, stir in the
fruit, nuts and mayonnaise. When just slightly set,
fold in the cream which has been whipped with the
salt. Gently stir in the Seven-Up. Mold and let set
overnight. Other fruit may be added such as
bananas or seedless grapes. If made without
the bananas, this salad will keep for several days.

CABBAGE-CARROT SALAD
Serves 4-6

½ cup mayonnaise
1 tablespoon lemon juice
2 teaspoons prepared mustard
¾ teaspoon salt
3 cups shredded cabbage
1 cup grated carrots
½ cup raisins

Combine mayonnaise, lemon juice, mustard and
salt. Mix with cabbage, carrots and raisins. Toss.

December

SUNDAY	MONDAY	TUESDAY	WEDNESDAY	THURSDAY	FRIDAY	SATURDAY
						1
2 FIRST SUNDAY OF ADVENT	3	4	5	6	7	8
9	10	11	12	13	14	15
16	17	18	19	20	21 HANUKKAH	22 WINTER BEGINS
23 / 30	24 / 31	25 CHRISTMAS DAY	26	27	28	29

Designing a calendar around variations of a theme has challenging possibilities.

Courtesy, Looart Press, Inc.

Designed by Roy Wilson

CHAPTER 9
STUDIO CARDS
BY
ROY WILSON

"Ours is a ticklish business" — Slogan for William Box Greeting Cards

Roughly one out of every fifteen Americans sends a printed, mass-produced sentiment to express his emotions. Years ago Americans sent greeting cards only to celebrate a few traditional holidays. Today we celebrate everything — even Halloween. To a recently unemployed friend, we sent a card showing two decrepit-looking bums on a park bench with a space between them and the verbal barb, "Welcome Back."

One card, designed by cartoonist William Box (considered the originator of the contemporary card), is an all-time best seller. The front of the card contains an assortment of sweet, romantic, typographic sentiments such as "Lover," "Sweetheart," "Fly to Me in Sweet Rapture," "You Are Mine," "All Mine." However, when you turn the page, you are hit with this cynicism, "Burn This." To a vacationing associate, we send a missive depicting a galley filled with dozens of weary slaves tugging at the oars with the inside caption, "Missing you at work." Obviously, the popularity of these cards indicates that the habits of the American public have undergone a transformation. Along with this, the greeting card itself has changed. A new type of card has emerged — the studio card, the card for any and alll occasions. In contrast to the ornate, sentimental traditional cards (often referred to as the fuzzy bunny school of art), the humor of the studio card is more satirical and often more sophisticated in appearance. Actually the studio card, with its offbeat, acerbic humor attuned to the emotional climate of the nuclear age, was long overdue. For too many years, people had been sending the traditional flowery congratulatory cards to newlyweds.

Lately, there has been a tendency to cross-breed the traditional card with the studio card. Sometimes it is difficult to tell the two apart. For example, you may even find an occasional sentimental verse on a studio card or prose and contemporary art work on a traditional card. Now that all the major card companies have a studio card line, they are using more the industry's favorite techniques, chopped cellophane that simulates the glitter of snow, paper that suggests the appearance of animal fur, and embossing-devices usually referred to in the trade by the colorful terms of flitter, flocking and bump-up.

It seems incredible, but greeting cards account for half of all the mail that people send each other. Small wonder that it has often been referred to as the "canned emotion" industry. Obviously, this enormous quantity of cards is going to keep a lot of printers on a busy schedule, along with many disgruntled mailmen. The choice of lithography for greeting card production is dictated by the nature of the greeting card design. This means considering the use of fine screens, softly vignetted illustrations, and papers ranging from matte to high gloss and antiques to vegetable parchment. Fuzzy and glossy finishes, die cutting and other special effects make it absolutely necessary for the greeting card printer to use a variety of printing techniques. Each card design may have as few as two or as many as five finishing operations.

Designed by Roy Wilson

This is a fine example of how both inside pages can be used to add impact to the punch line.

Designed by Roy Wilson

Using a real map gave this card more spark and personality.

Compared to most printers, the greeting card manufacturer occupies a somewhat unenviable position: he must produce his product before he can sell it. He must attempt to forecast public taste at the time the cards will be marketed, a difficult task in our cosmopolitan society even if you have a crystal ball. When the cards are finally engraved, printed and distributed, the public response to the new designs is anxiously awaited. Will sales be lost because of under-production or will over-production and unsold cards make red tracks on the profit and loss statement?

Most people are more or less reticent in their daily lives. They don't go around telling people, even their own families, how much they love, admire or appreciate them, even though they feel this way. But they do buy greeting cards to say it for them.

There are other reasons, rather obvious ones, why they purchase cards. It's easier. Also, Johnny probably can't write or doesn't like to write. Years ago people took great pleasure in writing and in receiving letters. Now letter writing is virtually obsolete. Apparently, many Johnnies and Janes can't and won't read either. This is evident by the fact that the picture plays the dominant role in the content of most cards. Visual symbols pervade our culture. Occasionally, a greeting card will not have an illustration, but even then the message will consist of only a few words of basic English, fewer words than a gumwrapper.

Perhaps greeting cards, with their little printed messages which are often funny, often hostile, sometimes witty, mirror the emotional state of large sectors of our frantic society. Who knows? In future years, these billions of cards may be the most definitive comment made about our culture.

Studio cards derive their name from the first ones which were created by some young artists living in Greenwich Village studios. Unable to sell their paintings, they designed original cards in India ink on white paper and sold them to the local gift shops. As the public acceptance of these cards increased, the purchasers insisted on envelopes also. Rather than incur additional expenses, the artists adapted their designs to an oblong format to accommodate the less expensive business envelope. Studio cards are generally inexpensive and rely on a funny gag written in prose style. The lead line is indicated on page one of the four page fold and the punch-line or surprise appears on page three.

AND

MERRY
CHRISTMAS
FROM
YOUR
AVANT-GARDE
FRIENDS
WAY OUT
HERE......

Designed by Roy Wilson

The accordian fold can add to the versatility of the layout and use of copy.

These cards successfully combine the humor of the studio card with the traditional approach.

In many cases the cover graphics can tell the whole story.

When studio cards were first introduced on a mass scale, not everyone liked them. William Box, who created some of the most original, caustic cards in this line, recalls that one stationer returned his first order of the cards with this comment, "I will not display your cards to any human."

The eventual success of the studio card proved that the people who disapproved were in the minority. Surprisingly, the rise of the studio card did not diminish the sale and continuing popularity of the traditional card. The contemporary card did not win over the previous card buying public as much as it created an entirely new market. People who had never bought a card before in their lives were now buying studio cards.

Recently, I saw a cartoon that portrayed a rather forlorn-looking middle-aged woman standing in front of a greeting card display asking the somewhat apprehensive clerk, "Have you anything for a man who just had a vasectomy?" Actually, she would not have to look far. Studio cards utilize practically every theme. Most of the traditional taboos have vanished. Nowadays we make fun of everything and everybody.

A wad of cotton, a few squiggly lines and provocative balloon copy on the cover followed by a tag line inside, combine to make an effective gag card.

Humor — biting, mischievous, impudent, sardonic — is the mainstay of the studio card. To a manufacturer of studio cards, this presents a problem since our taste in humor changes almost as rapidly as our fashions in clothes. They have to be aware of constant shifts in public taste. Studio cards are entertainment and like other forms of mass entertainment (the movies, television) their subject matter often involves walking a thin line between sophistication and vulgarity.

Studio cards, as they exist today, have branched out in several directions. Their appearance has changed rather than their content. The cards are still offering the sender a harmless therapeutic outlet for his dissatisfaction with social conformity. Only now, the cards come in all sizes and prices. In a society obsessed with status, I suppose this is inevitable. Anyway, if you have ten dollars, you can now buy a huge card decorated with fake mink or rhinestones to impress someone. Perhaps H. L. Menken was right when he remarked "Never underestimate the taste of the American public." There is plenty of evidence to substantiate his viewpoint in the greeting card racks.

In addition to your own drawing, take advantage of collage material. A magazine clipping here, an old photo there, helps give the design more emphasis and individuality. Remember, however, that if you pick up halftone copy, it will have to be screened by the engraver before it can be reproduced.

BIBLIOGRAPHY

GENERAL TECHNIQUE:

Biegeleisen, J.I.
Screen Printing
Watson-Guptill Publications, 1971

Haffer, Virna
Making Photograms
Amphoto-Hastings House, 1969

Laliberte, Norman and
Mogelon, Alex
Painting With Crayons
Van Nostrand Reinhold, 1967

Laliberte, Norman and
Mogelon, Ales
The Art of Stencil
Van Nostrand Reinhold, 1971

Mayer, Mary Jane and Webb, Mary
New Ways in Collage
Van Nostrand Reinhold, 1973

Romano, Clare and Ross, John,
The Complete Printmaker
The Free Press, 1972

Stevens, Harold
Design in Photo-Collage
Van Nostrand Reinhold, 1967

Meyer, Franz Sales
Handbook of Ornament
Dover Publications, Inc., 1957

TYPES OF DESIGN:

Ferebee, Ann
*A History of Design from the Victorian
Era to the Present*
Van Nostrand Reinhold, 1970

COMMERCIAL REPRODUCTION:

Ballinger, Raymond A.
Layout and Graphic Design
Van Nostrand Reinhold, 1970

Gates, David
Lettering for Reproduction
Watson-Guptill Publications, 1969

Stone, Bernard and Eckstein, Arthur
Preparing Art for Printing
Van Nostrand Reinhold, 1965

SOURCES

ART SUPPLIES, ALL KINDS:

Arthur Brown and Bros. Inc.
2 West 46 Street
New York, N.Y. 10036

Dick Blick Co.
P.O. Box 1267
Galesburg, ILL. 61401

Dixie Art Supplies, Inc.
420 Julia Street
New Orleans, LA. 70130

Flax's Artist's Materials
1699 Market Street
San Francisco, CA. 94108

SPECIALTY ITEMS:

AZOCOL DIRECT EMULSION:

Colonial Printing Ink Co.
Division of U.S. Printing Ink Corp.
180 E. Union Ave.
East Rutherford, N.J. 07073

BLOCK PRINTING PAPER:

Technical Papers Corp.
29 Franklin Street
Needham, MA. 02194

LINOLEUM TOOLS:

Bergen Arts and Crafts
P.O. Box 381, 14 Prospect St.
Marblehead, MA. 01945

NOVELTY PAPER, PLASTIC, AND BEAD ITEMS:

Dennison Manufacturing Company
370 Lexington Avenue
New York, N.Y. 10017

PRINTMAKING SUPPLIES:

Graphic Chemical and Ink Co.
728 North Yale Avenue
Villa Park, ILL. 60181

INDEX